D0371987

YOU ARE THE EXPLORER

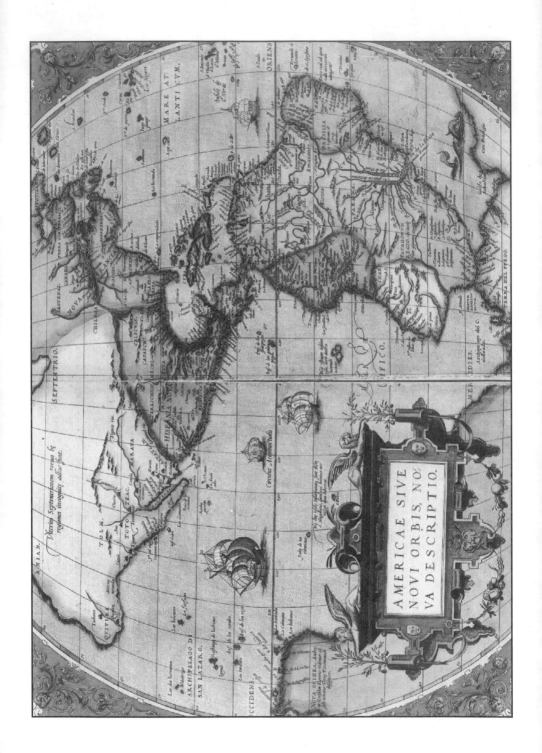

GREAT DECISIONS

YOU
ARE THE
EXPLORER

Nathan Aaseng

The Oliver Press, Inc.
Minneapolis

Page 2: *Abraham Ortelius's 1570 map of the New World from his book,* Theatrum orbis terrarum (Theater of the World), *generally considered the world's first great atlas*

Copyright © 2000 by The Oliver Press, Inc.
All rights reserved.
No part of this book may be reproduced in any form or by any means without permission in writing from the publisher.
Please address inquiries to:

The Oliver Press, Inc.
Charlotte Square
5707 West 36th Street
Minneapolis, MN 55416-2510

Library of Congress Cataloging-in-Publication Data

Aaseng, Nathan.
You are the explorer / Nathan Aaseng.
p.   cm.—(Great decisions)
Includes bibliographical references and index.
    Summary: Discusses the decisions faced by such explorers as Christopher Columbus, James Cook, Samuel de Champlain, and Robert Scott, offers options these men needed to consider, and analyzes the courses of action they chose.
ISBN 1-881508-55-2 (lib. bdg.)
1. Discoveries in geography—Juvenile literature. 2. Explorers—Juvenile literature. [1. Explorers. 2. Discoveries in geography. 3. Decision making.] I. Title. II. Series: Great decisions (Minneapolis, Minn.).
G175.A18 1999
910'.92'2—dc21   98-50136
                                                                    CIP
                                                                     AC

ISBN: 1-881508-55-2
Great Decisions IX
Printed in the United States of America

06 05 04 03 02 01 00   8 7 6 5 4 3 2 1

CONTENTS

21.00

Bond Money

11-26-01

LIBRARY
DEXTER SCHOOLS
DEXTER, NM 88230

An astrolabe was one of the instruments explorers of the past used to determine their latitude. A navigator held the device from the ring and lined up the arms to point to the horizon and either the sun or North Star. Unfortunately, it was not always accurate, especially when used aboard a rocking ship at sea.

INTRODUCTION

Say goodbye to safety and security. From now until the end of your journey, a world of danger, mystery, and challenge surrounds you.

You have cast off on a mission to explore a part of the earth that no one from your culture has ever seen. You will sail into vast, uncharted oceans far from sight of any land. You will strike off into forests and mountains and icy glaciers without any sure idea of what lies ahead. You will encounter tense situations with natives whose customs are completely foreign to you.

Throughout all these adventures, you are in charge. Responsibility lies heavily upon you. By disappearing into the unknown, you have left behind any possibility that someone can rescue you. You and your crew will live or die with the consequences of any decision you make.

In some ways, your responsibilities are greater than those of any king, queen, or emperor on earth. Explorers live on the cutting edge of history. With a simple command, you can change the course of world events and alter forever the lives of millions of people. The choices

Juan Ponce de León (1460-1521) was one of a number of Spaniards looking to gain wealth and land for his country in the New World. He discovered Florida while searching for gold.

you make could determine whether your nation succeeds or fails in the race for colonies and trade routes.

Yet often you have scanty information on which to base these important decisions. You could end up making what seems like a reasonable choice only to discover serious consequences that you had no way of anticipating.

An explorer needs many of the qualities that most capable leaders require. You will have to be a good judge of character. There is a limit to how much danger, hardship, and uncertainty your crew members can endure. Sometimes, you will need to encourage them; other times, you will have to drive them against their will. But you will need to be careful. If you push your crew beyond its breaking point, disaster is certain.

An explorer must have nerves of steel. There will be times when the terror of the unknown will gnaw at you, when unseen misfortunes will cast doubt on the wisdom of your actions. You must have the courage to stand by your convictions when all others think you are crazy.

On the other hand, you will also need sound judgment. Even the boldest explorer cannot afford to proceed recklessly against all odds. Explorers who vanish into the unknown and are never heard from again accomplish nothing. You will have to know when to hold fast to a course of action and when to adapt to new situations.

An explorer must have shrewd political sense. Your expedition could stumble upon a vast fortune, and there

The English navigator Henry Hudson did not know when to give up on searching for the Northwest Passage through the Americas. His crew eventually left him and eight others to die in Canada's Hudson Bay in 1611.

In 1519, the Spanish explorer Vasco Núñez de Balboa was beheaded by his government on unsubstantiated charges made by his enemies—just a few years after he claimed the Pacific Ocean for Spain.

are many greedy and powerful people back home waiting to get their hands on it. They are eager for an excuse to accuse you of being incompetent or a traitor so that they can win the riches and glory that are rightfully yours.

Finally, an explorer must be lucky. You do not know exactly what lies ahead. In many cases you simply will have to rely on instinct and hope for the best.

The eight explorers' dilemmas that follow take you into the Atlantic, Pacific, and Indian Oceans, to the powerful civilizations and vast forests of the Americas, and to the frozen wastes of Antarctica. In each case, a wrong decision could bring about the ruin of the expedition and make your name synonymous with failure for eternity. But a correct decision could bring tremendous rewards.

Bon voyage!

1

THE TERROR OF THE ENDLESS OCEAN
1492

You have just sailed out of sight of the Canary Islands, the last known land as you sail west into the vast Atlantic Ocean. Now all you can see in any direction is water.

You are attempting a voyage that no one else has ever dared. You are trying to sail west across the Atlantic to the exotic lands of parts of China, India, and other Asian territories known as the Indies. If all goes well, you should reach the Indies in a matter of weeks—according to your calculations. But these calculations are only educated guesses. No one you know of has ever actually sailed so far directly into the open Atlantic. What lies ahead is uncertain. Since you must rely heavily upon a

After many months at sea with only crude instruments to guide them, sailors of the fifteenth century often imagine horrifying sea monsters and invent other myths.

compass, and little more, to help you figure out where you are and what direction you are heading, you could easily get lost in such a huge ocean.

As the Canary Islands disappear from sight, the signs of tension are obvious. Many of the crew appear frightened, and a few are weeping in terror. Their attitude is not likely to improve the farther you sail into the unknown. A strong possibility exists that they will lose heart completely and demand that you turn for home.

For years, you have been pleading for the chance to make this voyage. Every educated person knows the world is round. Therefore, by traveling west, you will eventually reach the East. In pioneering this route to the Indies, you could establish a fabulously rich trade in spices.

No one knows what lies in the way of such a voyage or whether one can keep a steady course on such a long voyage out of sight of land. But the key issue is distance. How far must one sail west before reaching the Indies?

The calculations of the respected ancient geographer Ptolemy put the circumference of the earth at

The ancient Greek Ptolemy, shown here at left, was an astronomer, geographer, and mathematician. On the right is Euclid, a highly respected Greek mathematician.

roughly 20,000 miles. Ptolemy also determined one-half of the earth to be ocean. Through further investigation, you concluded the earth is made up of even less water. Based on this, and on maps of Asia, you estimate the distance from western Europe across the Atlantic Ocean to Japan is 2,400 miles. The distance to China, the most likely source of rich trade, would be about 3,500 miles. Given the favorable winds that you hope will blow all the way across the Atlantic, this is a reasonable distance for a well-made ship to travel.

Unfortunately, not everyone agrees with your figures. When you proposed your voyage to King Ferdinand and Queen Isabella of Spain, they consulted a panel of experts. These experts claimed that the distance across the Atlantic was much greater than you figured. Such a voyage, they concluded, was impractical. Only with the influence of friends, and a lot of persuasion, were you able to convince Spain of backing your voyage.

Most of your crew members are not well educated. They have numerous fears and age-old superstitions about the uncharted ocean to the west. The longer they are out at sea, the more their fears will grow.

The fact that this is a Spanish expedition complicates your relations with your crew. The crew is Spanish, and you are not. For most of your career, you have sailed for Portugal, Spain's major seafaring rival. You would be sailing for them still had not the Portuguese rejected your proposal for this ocean voyage. Not surprisingly, most of the crew members are wary of you. They have come aboard solely because they trust Martin Pinzon, who has signed on as captain of one of your three ships.

After much persuasion, King Ferdinand of Spain
agreed to back your voyage to the Indies.

This is a potentially explosive situation. Out on the high seas, far from any government authority, disgruntled sailors are often tempted to overthrow their leaders, an event known as mutiny.

THE DECISION IS YOURS.

How will you deal with a nervous and distrustful crew to guarantee that they will not lose courage, mutiny, and turn back for home?

Option 1 **Rule with an iron fist.**

Even though you are not Spanish, you are the leader of this expedition. So act like it. Remind the crew that their king and queen personally authorized you to take charge of these ships. Your orders, therefore, are the king and queen's orders. Let the crew know, without question, that your mission is to sail to the Indies—and that you intend to do so, no matter what.

Griping tends to be contagious. Inform the crew that you will tolerate no grumbling, whining, or complaining. To make sure that none of this discontent spreads, squash it the instant it appears. As commander of the fleet, you have virtually unlimited authority to enforce discipline. If you deal out strong punishments to the first gripers, you will make an example of them that will discourage others from displaying a low morale. They may not like you for this, but they will respect you.

Once you have reached the Indies, and the men realize what riches and glory they have earned, they will thank you for your strong stand.

Option 2 **Agree at the start to sail a certain number of miles and no farther.**

As a foreigner leading a Spanish crew, you had better be careful how you treat your sailors. They do not trust you. Their loyalty is to Martin Pinzon. If they sense that you are leading them to their doom, harsh punishments will not deter them from overthrowing you. In fact, if they felt you were overly brutal and unfair, they would be all the more likely to get rid of you. Pinzon is an ambitious person who may well be tempted to take advantage of the situation and lead a takeover to gain the glory of the expedition for himself.

The main cause of unrest is the terror of the unknown. The sailors need some assurance that you know what you are doing and that their journey will end safely. Just telling them that you will sail until you reach land will not help. As weeks go by with no land in sight, the crew is going to wonder if they will ever see land again. For all they know, you could keep sailing until you starve or are lost forever. The best way to put the crew at ease is to set a limit on the voyage.

The fleet consists of three ships known as caravels, which are swift and maneuverable—yet small. After many months at sea, a cramped crew will want to know when they will land.

You have spent many years determining how far away the Indies must be. Since you believe the distance to China to be roughly 3,500 miles, give yourself a reasonable margin for error. But do not make the distance too far, or you will discourage the crew and defeat your whole purpose. Therefore, inform the crew that you will turn around if you have not found land by 3,750 miles.

This is a gamble. It means that you might come within a day or two of the Indies and have to turn back. But this whole voyage is a huge gamble. You have already bet your reputation that your calculations of the distance are correct. Stay with your convictions.

Option 3 **Trick your crew into believing they have traveled less far than they actually have.**

The problem with setting a target number of miles for the trip is that sailing unknown oceans is hardly an exact science. Although your research is based on the best information you have, you could still be off by a few hundred miles.

Suppose you reach your target distance without finding land. Your glorious voyage would then end in failure. How could you live with the nagging doubt that you might have come within a day or two of sighting the Indies only to have to turn back?

You think you have a pretty good idea of the distance to the Indies. But you must also plan for the possibility of sailing farther than the crew is willing to.

One way to accomplish this is to underestimate the distance you travel each day. The best available method for measuring rate of travel is very inaccurate. It basically involves throwing a stick attached to a string into the water, then measuring how much string follows the floating stick out the back of the ship in an hour. As captain of the fleet, you are in charge of using this method and your own estimations to determine how far you have traveled. Each day, tell your crew that you have sailed 10 to 40 miles less than you actually have. After several weeks, you will be able to convince the crew and the other two captains that you have traveled only 3,500 miles when you have actually gone 4,000.

As you get close to where the Indies ought to be, you should be able to point out signs that land is near. Certain species of birds, fish, and plants that you may encounter live near land. You can probably squeeze a few days more of sailing out of a reluctant crew by pointing out these signs of hope.

There is one problem with this option. If the crew ever found out what you were doing, they would not hesitate to overthrow you. You *are* Portuguese, and deceiving your crew is not the way to win their trust and support.

Option 4 Look for islands along the way.

Your goal is the Indies and the rich spice trade that this will bring. You think you know where this land lies, but you cannot be certain. If you do not find the Indies where you expect them to be, you might want to think about salvaging your voyage another way—by discovering previously unknown islands.

No one in Europe knows for certain what might lie between the Canary Islands and the Indies. Perhaps there are no islands of any interest out in the Atlantic. But after traveling thousands of miles in a seemingly endless ocean, the crew may be desperate for the sight of land. Even if an island does not hold the spices and trade you desire, it is land. You may need to stop there to save the crew's sanity.

The Portuguese have often found islands in the ocean by following the flight patterns of certain birds. As you get far out into the ocean, all you need to do is stay alert for birds who do not fly great distances and follow them to land. You could be discovering new lands full of gold and other riches. On the other hand, you might end up wasting time in a search for what prove to be insignificant and barren lands.

A tern is a bird that many believe does not stray far from land. You should encounter terns either towards the end of your journey or when other land is nearby.

Don't forget that according to your calculations, you should come across the large island of Japan at 2,400 miles. If you do not reach it by then, it may be a good indication that your measurements are off. At that point, it would be the right time to start searching for other islands.

YOU ARE THE EXPLORER.
WHAT IS YOUR DECISION?

Option 1   Rule with an iron fist.

Option 2   Agree at the start to sail a certain number of miles and no farther.

Option 3   Trick your crew into believing they have traveled less far than they actually have.

Option 4   Look for islands along the way.

Christopher Columbus (1451-1506) began his sailing career around the age of 14 as a pirate. He later fought battles at sea for Portugal and sailed to places as far away as Iceland before setting his famous course west for the Indies.

Christopher Columbus chose *Option 3*.

Columbus was obsessed with finding a fast, easy route to Asia. He spent years trying to persuade wealthy rulers to finance this experimental voyage. Now that he finally had his ships, he intended to sail west until he hit Asia or died trying. "My goal is the Indies and it would make no sense to waste time with offshore islands," he wrote, and so he rejected *Option 4*.

Although Columbus had strong faith in his calculations, many of the sources were in disagreement. He knew he could be off by several hundred miles. Given the uncertainty over the distance, he refused to risk the entire expedition by setting a limit on how far they would sail, rejecting *Option 2*.

Also, Columbus was concerned about his position as a foreign leader of a Spanish crew. He thought that using harsh punishments to force the crew to bend to his will (*Option 1*) would probably lead to mutiny. The wisest course, he decided, was to deceive his crew.

In his log book, Columbus kept two figures. One was the distance he calculated they had traveled that day. The other was a smaller distance that he reported to the crew. "I decided to count less than I was covering," he wrote in his log, "so that if the voyage should be long, the crew would not grow afraid or disheartened." For example, on September 10 he told the crew they had sailed 144 miles, when he calculated 180 miles.

As the voyage dragged on, Columbus looked for plants and animals found only near land. He kept finding reasons why they should sail just a little farther.

RESULT

As Columbus feared, he began to have trouble with the crew. They were particularly worried about the strong east winds that constantly blew them into the unknown. If the wind always came from the east, how would they ever get home? In late September, a few of Columbus's trusted men told him that the rest of the crew members were unhappy and even planning to mutiny if the expedition did not find land soon.

But the ships sailed on, and Columbus continued to underestimate the true distance. He tried to relieve the crew's anxiety by telling them stories of how rich they would become once they reached the Indies. Columbus pointed to flocks of flying birds, certain crabs and seaweed in the water, passing pods of whales, and the smoothness of the water as evidence that land was near. Columbus was so convincing, and the men so desperate to believe him, that the sailors falsely sighted land several times.

But by early October, the expedition had traveled about 2,500 miles without running into Japan or any other part of Asia. At this point, the crew saw many birds flying to the southwest. Martin Pinzon advised Columbus to follow the birds toward what he was convinced was land. Columbus boldly replied, "My calculations do not indicate that land is in that direction, and I am not going to waste time with it." The next day, under pressure, Columbus had a change of heart and turned course to the southwest.

Columbus kept insisting that land was near. "If we do not find land you are permitted to cut off my head;

that way you can sail home in peace," he told them. But as time dragged on, some of the crew members might have been tempted to take him up on his offer.

Several days after changing course, the men came across branches with berries and other signs of nearby land. At 2 A.M. on October 12, they sighted land at last.

After this voyage, Columbus completed three other trips across the Atlantic. He went to his death believing he had succeeded in his life's mission—finding a shorter route to the Indies. In fact, his expedition had stumbled upon an entire continent that it never knew existed.

When Columbus and his crew landed in the Caribbean, they were eager to trade with the natives—not the other way around, as this picture suggests.

ANALYSIS

Columbus's decision to trick his crew helped bring about one of the most important voyages of all time. His journey ushered in an era of European exploration of vast lands and new cultures that dramatically altered the lives of millions of people.

Columbus's strategy helped make this all possible. It allowed him to keep his reluctant crew on task and avoid a mutiny. Had he tried to impose strict discipline on the crew, the result could well have been different.

The success of his voyage, however, was largely a matter of luck. As the experts of Portugal and Spain had insisted, Columbus was far off in his calculations of the distance across the Atlantic to China. The actual distance to his destination turned out to be not 3,500 miles but over 11,000! Given that fact, he would probably have been wiser to turn back after a certain distance or attempt to discover and explore islands. Had the unsuspected American continent not happened to be in the way, no amount of deception or stalling would have saved Columbus. He undoubtedly would have lost control of his crew long before he reached the Indies.

In other words, Columbus's decision to trick his crew turned his expedition into a huge success, even though he was looking for an entirely different continent.

2

ROUNDING THE COAST OF AFRICA
1497

Spices from the Indies are so valuable that they will make the European country that controls the spice trade one of the richest nations in the world. The current trade route to the Indies, lands that make up parts of South, Southeast, and East Asia, goes through the Mediterranean Sea and across lands controlled by Arabs. For many years, your country, Portugal, has been sending ships down the west coast of Africa in the hope of finding a direct sea route to the Indies and these spices. This would enable Portugal to obtain the spices for only a fraction of the current price by eliminating the middleman. About 10 years ago, one of these explorers, Bartolomeu Diaz, finally located open waters

*When Bartolomeu Diaz (1450?-1500) finally
reached the southern tip of Africa, he planted a cross
there and held a special service to mark the occasion.*

off the southern tip of Africa. There appears to be no
land mass barring the way of an ocean voyage from
Portugal around the southern tip of Africa to the Indies.

Your mission is to build on what Diaz has accomplished. You are to establish a trade route by being the
first to sail around Africa to India, the westernmost source
of trade in the Indies.

Your most important decisions may occur before
you ever leave port. You will need to decide what type of
ship you want to use and what route you will take to reach
the southern coast of Africa efficiently.

BACKGROUND

Portuguese sailors can provide you with a great deal of information about what to expect on the first part of your journey. They have been sailing into the Atlantic Ocean and down the African coast for many years.

One of the nagging frustrations they have experienced on these African voyages has been the southerly winds and currents along the coast near the equator. All ocean-going ships of the late fifteenth century depend on the wind and ocean current to provide power. A relatively short journey down the African coast can drag out into many weeks if you are sailing against a strong wind.

Another problem awaits you further along. Diaz is the only commander you know to sail in the waters off the

Portuguese prince Henry the Navigator (1394-1460) set up a school of navigation and sponsored many voyages south along the African coast to find a sea route to the Indies.

southern coast of Africa. He reports extremely rough seas in that area.

Diaz sailed in swift vessels known as caravels. Caravels have a shallow draft—that is, they float high in the water. The advantages of this type of ship are that it can sail quickly and can maneuver well enough to stick close to the coast without getting caught on dangerous rocks. One of the disadvantages is that it is not as stable as heavier ships when caught in stormy seas and strong winds. It also has less storage room. Diaz solved the problem of limited storage by sending ahead a large, slow supply ship prior to his fleet's departure. The supply ship waited for Diaz's fleet halfway down the coast of Africa. Diaz and his crew then loaded up on supplies both on their way down the coast of Africa and on their return trip home.

Over the years, sailors have made some advances in navigation by using the stars and several crude instruments. Nonetheless, all previous voyages south along the coast of Africa have stayed near land to help the navigators keep their bearings.

THE DECISION IS YOURS.

What type of ships will you use and what route will you take in your voyage around Africa to the Indies?

Option 1 **Use caravels; stay along the coast.**
Stay with the tried-and-true caravels. Basically, you are using the route pioneered by Diaz, who had success with caravels and a supply ship. Why not follow his lead?

The caravel, such as the one in this fifteenth-century illustration, has a round bottom and sits high in the water. It is designed for speed and maneuverability.

Caravels are fast ships. This could be a very long voyage, especially if you have to fight headwinds and currents. You don't want to make it any longer by sailing in slow, heavy ships. The caravels' shallow bottoms will also help prevent you from getting shipwrecked on submerged rocks near the coast.

A supply ship will not slow you down if you send it out beforehand and have it wait for you at the southern tip of Africa. You can have this ship remain at the same spot where it will be waiting to resupply you on your return voyage from the Indies.

Some may argue that caravels are too small and unstable to send out on such a long trip into the unknown and possibly rough waters that lie beyond Africa. But remember that Christopher Columbus crossed the great Atlantic Ocean in caravels. His ships were sturdy enough to survive a tremendous storm on the way home.

As for the route, navigation is your utmost concern. By remaining near the coastline, you can easily keep your bearings. You can also dash for the safety of a harbor should a dangerous storm blow in. Heading far out into the Atlantic puts you at risk of losing your way and falling victim to the weather.

Furthermore, although reports from Portuguese sailors indicate that you are likely to find more favorable winds out in the Atlantic, there is no guarantee of this. You could sail hundreds of miles out of your way for nothing. Worse yet, the winds could be so strong and northerly that they push you past the southern coast of Africa. You could end up floundering in unknown seas at the bottom of the world.

A crosstaff is one of several crude devices available to estimate latitude. Its use involves sliding the shorter stick along the longer one to line up the ends of the shorter stick with either the sun or North Star and the horizon. (Not easily done aboard a rocking ship.) Markings on the longer stick lead to judging latitude.

Option 2 Use caravels; head out into the Atlantic.

Use the caravels for the above reasons. But do you really want to spend long weeks, even months, battling against the currents along the coast?

There is a good chance that you will find more favorable conditions for your trip down to the southern coast of Africa if you sweep far out into the Atlantic. Bartolomeu Diaz's experience supports this idea. While slogging at a snail's pace against the winds along the African coast, Diaz noticed a fairly strong wind blowing from the west, a few miles away from shore. Towards the southern tip of Africa, he ran into strong winds originating from the northwest. They were so strong that they

LIBRARY
DEXTER SCHOOLS
DEXTER, NM 88230

blew Diaz far to the south of the coastline—so far, in fact, that he almost missed finding the coast at all. If this is a common weather pattern in that area of the world, you might expect those west and northwest winds to originate far out in the Atlantic.

Think of the time you would save if you found those winds. Although the distance you sail might be greater than if you stayed along the coast, favorable winds and currents could very well carry you to your destination much more quickly. The time you save would be well worth the risk of difficult navigation and bad weather.

Option 3 Take larger ships; stay along the coast.

Stay along the coast for the navigational concerns mentioned in **Option 1**, but don't take caravels.

Sending a supply ship out ahead to wait for the rest of the ships is not exactly foolproof. It can be dangerous to leave a handful of men to bide time and fend for themselves in foreign places. Diaz, for example, came upon a horrible disaster when he returned to his supply ship after reaching the southern coast of Africa. Only three of the crew members left on the supply ship were still alive, and one of those died shortly thereafter. The other six had been killed by natives. Your journey is much farther and will leave the supply crews stranded for a lot longer than Diaz's. Furthermore, trying to coordinate linking up with a supply ship over such long distances and time periods could prove difficult.

Given this situation, you would do better to keep your whole crew together and carry all your supplies with you for the entire journey. Since you would be traveling in slower ships, your supply ship can come along with you. When you reach the southern tip of Africa, you can load up your other ships with the contents of the supply ship and then sink it. From there, you can sail on to India, where you will resupply for the return trip. Because you will now know the distance and way back, you can accurately gauge the amount of supplies needed.

Another consideration is the stability of the caravels. Diaz found the seas along the southern tip of Africa so violent that he named the place the Cape of Storms (later named the Cape of Good Hope). Even he wonders about the wisdom of sending shallow-bottomed, top-heavy caravels back into those waters.

At the Cape of Good Hope, Diaz found the winds and sea to be violent. With rocky cliffs nearby, this could be a deadly combination for the wrong type of ship.

A larger ship, such as this one, can be designed to resemble the caravel but built bigger to provide more stability in stormy weather. Still, it would be slower and more cumbersome than the caravel.

Option 4 **Take larger ships; head out into the Atlantic.**

Option 3 gives sound reasons for taking larger ships on your voyage. But the use of larger ships is even more reason for heading out into the Atlantic. These larger ships are slower than the caravels. The caravels had trouble making headway against the winds and currents along the coast. Your heavier ships would find the going even tougher. The larger ships are made for going out into the ocean for long stretches at sea. You still would be faced with the problem of navigation and finding favorable winds, but you will have more supplies on board. Even if you had trouble at sea, your margin for error is greater.

YOU ARE THE EXPLORER.
WHAT IS YOUR DECISION?

Option 1   **Use caravels; stay along the coast.**

Option 2   **Use caravels; head out into the Atlantic.**

Option 3   **Take larger ships; stay along the coast.**

Option 4   **Take larger ships; head out into the Atlantic.**

Although an accomplished sailor, Vasco da Gama (1460?-1525) was not the captain originally appointed to lead the fleet around Africa to the Indies—his father was. Vasco was chosen when Estêvão da Gama died before the journey was to begin.

Vasco da Gama chose *Option 4*.

Da Gama listened carefully to Diaz's descriptions of his tiny ship battling huge waves that threatened to engulf it at the Cape of Storms. He decided that he needed larger, deeper-hulled ships to ensure safe passage. These ships could carry more crew members, food, water, and other supplies than a caravel. They were more suited for a journey of this length.

Da Gama was familiar with the common Portuguese complaints about the monotonous, slow sailing against the winds and currents along the western coast of Africa. Fearful of getting bogged down for months along the coast, he decided to take a gamble. His plan was to strike out hundreds of miles from the African shoreline into the Atlantic in a wide sweep that he hoped would find favorable winds that would blow him to southern Africa.

RESULT

On July 8, 1497, da Gama sailed out of Portugal with approximately 150 men in four ships: two special-made, deep-bottomed ships, one supply ship, and one caravel to support the others. They passed the Cape Verde Islands at the beginning of August. But instead of sailing east and then south along the coast, as the Portuguese had done for more than 75 years, he ordered the ships to continue to the south, away from the coast.

Having made his decision, da Gama stuck boldly to it. His search for the westerly winds led him hundreds of miles south into the Atlantic Ocean. By going so many months without sighting land, da Gama risked getting lost. By the time he found the westerly winds, he had only a rough idea of his location.

The westerlies drove the four ships to the east at a fast clip. Vasco da Gama spotted the African coast on November 4. His navigation proved to be brilliant. His ships landed at Helena Bay, only 150 miles north of the Cape of Good Hope.

Da Gama sailed around the cape and, according to plan, loaded up his other three ships with the contents of the supply ship and sank it. He then continued up the eastern coast of Africa and into the Indian Ocean. Several months later, with the help of an Arab navigator he had obtained in the port of Malindi, his ships reached India.

After over nine months at sea, Vasco da Gama's ships finally reached Calicut, India, on May 20, 1498.

Unfortunately, da Gama and Portugal had poor business sense. He brought only cheap trinkets to trade, which only insulted his trading partners. As a result, the voyage not only failed to bring him the expected riches, but actually lost money. Furthermore, by the time the explorer reached home two years later, he had lost one of his three remaining ships and over half his crew.

Nonetheless, he completed his mission of establishing an all-water route to the Far East. Da Gama returned to Portugal a hero and received money and lofty titles as his reward.

ANALYSIS

Da Gama's strategy of using larger boats and sailing into the Atlantic proved a success. He completed his important mission and found a safer and faster way to travel to the southern coast of Africa. Portugal did, eventually, acquire tremendous wealth from its all-water trade route to the Far East. Also, although da Gama's expedition lost most of its crew (mainly to a disease called scurvy), those losses could be expected for an expedition of that length at that time.

Had da Gama taken caravels instead, he might have run into the same problems Diaz had in leaving a supply ship to wait or battling winds at the Cape of Good Hope. By taking larger ships, da Gama was also able to take more supplies with him from the Cape of Good Hope to India.

The Atlantic sweep saved so much time and effort that later Portuguese voyages around Africa all followed

By sailing into the Atlantic Ocean instead of hugging the African coast on the first half of his journey, Vasco da Gama established a sea route to the Indies that the Portuguese would benefit from for years.

that route. Indirectly, da Gama's choice of routes helped Portugal establish itself in South America. His southern sweep into the Atlantic brought him within 600 miles of the coast of Brazil. Later Portuguese sailors following the same route sailed even farther into the Atlantic Ocean— far enough to discover this land. Soon, Brazil became a Portuguese colony, and to this day its dominant language is Portuguese.

3

FUGITIVE IN THE LAND
OF THE AZTECS
1520

Your ambition has gotten you into a dangerous mess. A year ago, you defied Governor Diego Velázquez's orders and sailed to Mexico with an expedition of 500 soldiers and 100 sailors. Expecting to find timid, primitive peoples to conquer, you instead encountered the mighty Aztec Empire.

A sensible person might have backed away from provoking a highly disciplined army of over 100,000, but you could not resist the lure of gold. Upon discovering an incredibly large store of gold in the Aztec capital of Tenochtitlán, you maneuvered your way into the city. At the moment, the Aztecs are not threatening you, mainly because you have succeeded in kidnapping their king,

You and your men have captured the Aztec king to provide insurance against an attack.

Moctezuma (or Montezuma), and are holding him hostage. But the situation is becoming tense.

Now comes word that Velázquez has sent an army much larger than yours to Mexico with orders to arrest you. How are you going to get out of this tight spot?

BACKGROUND

You used to be on good terms with Velázquez, the governor of Spain's colony of Cuba. In fact, Velázquez had originally appointed you to lead the expedition to Mexico. But you managed to put together such a powerful army that Velázquez grew jealous and had you dismissed from command. Fortunately, you heard about Velázquez's plans and set sail before he could take action against you.

Now, however, Velázquez has sent a 900-man army led by Pánfilo de Narváez to arrest you.

Up to this point, luck has been with you all the way. Shortly after landing in Mexico, you found a Spaniard named Aguilar who was shipwrecked off the shore of this land seven years ago. He has learned native languages of the people here and can help you communicate with them. Your small army was able to defeat a much larger force of Tlaxcalans, who were intimidated by your horses and guns. They had never seen either before. It so happens that the Tlaxcalans hate the powerful Aztec Empire because it oppresses them. They are willing to fight with you against the Aztecs, who still vastly outnumber you both.

Even with Tlaxcalan help, you will have great difficulty defeating the Aztecs. Their capital city of Tenochtitlán is surrounded by water. You can enter it only on narrow causeways that the Aztecs can easily defend. Again, though, you have had a lucky break. You happened to arrive in Mexico at about the time that the Aztec god Quetzalcoatl was expected to return to this land, according to Aztec astronomers. This coincidence, along with your firearms, horses, and strange appearance, has led the Aztecs to believe that you are children of the gods. They have brought you fabulous presents of gold in hopes that you will accept the gifts and not bring harm to them.

The presents, however, have only whetted your appetite for more riches. Secretly you started a fire that burned your 11 ships so that your men would be forced to follow you against this enormous army. With the Aztecs

Quetzalcoatl means "plumed serpent." He is the Aztec god of soil, vegetation, and the arts.

still hesitant to challenge a god, you marched into Tenochtitlán without firing a shot. As insurance against an Aztec uprising, you have taken their ruler, Moctezuma, hostage. One of the terms of his release is that the Aztecs must give you more gold. From what you have seen, they own more gold than any king or queen in Europe.

THE DECISION IS YOURS.

The arrival of Pánfilo de Narváez and his army has trapped you between two enemies. Narváez is coming to arrest you. The Aztecs, with their overwhelming numbers, could turn against you at any moment. How can you salvage the situation?

Like all Aztec kings, Moctezuma was selected to be king. The position was not automatically given to the first-born son of the previous ruler. However, Aztec kings are always chosen from the same family line.

Option 1 **Surrender yourself to Narváez.**

You are in an impossible spot, with strong enemies all around you. If you stay where you are, Narváez will come after you with a force larger than yours. The Aztecs cannot be counted on to help you against him. By kidnapping their leader, you have not exactly treated the Aztecs with kindness. They would most likely love nothing better than to see the strangers destroy themselves fighting each other. Even worse, once the Aztecs see the first of your men wounded in a battle with Narváez, they will realize that you are not gods and turn against you.

You don't have to fear Velázquez; after all, you were only following your original orders when you left for Mexico. Furthermore, when the governor of Cuba sees what you have accomplished, he will reward, not punish, you. Velázquez has always had a reputation for quickly forgiving people. Also, other Spanish explorers have been scouring the New World for gold, and you are one of the few to hit the jackpot.

Many of your men are urging you to do the sensible thing: quit while you are ahead. Surrender yourself to Narváez. You have already collected enough Aztec gold to make you and your men rich, with plenty left over to win the favor of Spanish officials.

Option 2 **Flee with the gold.**

For reasons given above, you cannot stay in Tenochtitlán, nor do you want to challenge Narváez. But you could be committing suicide if you surrender peaceably to Narváez. Leaving Cuba against Velázquez's orders was a serious offense, which he will probably consider to be treason. He must still be furious with you, or he would not have sent such a large expedition after you.

You also know that the Spanish government is full of people looking to make names for themselves at other peoples' expense. They have shown an eagerness to treat explorers badly to advance themselves. Even Christopher Columbus was thrown in jail after discovering the New World because of complaints about his behavior.

Worse yet, take the case of Vasco Núñez de Balboa. In 1513, he became the first European to see the Pacific Ocean and loyally claimed it for Spain. Six years later, his enemies in the Spanish government beheaded him on flimsy charges of corruption and treason.

Charles I of Spain (who also became Charles V of the Holy Roman Empire last year) was king of Spain when Balboa was beheaded. He still is king now.

You might well meet the same fate. Your best hope of staying alive and reasonably well off is to flee with your gold to another part of the New World. You could establish your own settlement with your newfound wealth.

Option 3 **Lead your entire army against Narváez.**

You risk prison or execution if you surrender to Narváez. Thanks to your rash decision to burn all your ships, you have no easy way of fleeing Mexico. You might have to wander hundreds or even thousands of miles through uncharted jungle, mountains, and deserts without a food supply.

Shortly after arriving in Mexico, you hauled all of your equipment to shore and burned your ships so that none of your men could back out of your expedition.

Your best hope of survival, then, is to defeat Pánfilo de Narváez. While you might be reluctant to leave Tenochtitlán after all the effort you have gone through to gain control of it, you have no choice. You cannot risk a confrontation with Narváez in front of the Aztecs. It would be far better to fight the battle off by the coast where the Aztecs won't see the "gods" bleed.

Nor can you leave any men behind to keep a foothold on Tenochtitlán. Even when you are at full strength, you are still outnumbered by Narváez. You will need every soldier under your command to fight a desperate battle for survival. Only after you have defeated Narváez can you turn your attention back towards the Aztec Empire.

Option 4 Send part of your force to deal with Narváez.

This is an extremely risky strategy, but the payoff will be tremendous if it works. The Aztec Empire is grander than any other civilization that has been found in the New World, and you are in a position to be the sole ruler of it.

Only by the most fortunate of circumstances were you able to enter the capital city without bloodshed. But Aztec mistrust of you is growing. They would love to be rid of you but are still confused as to how to go about it. Were you to leave the city, you can bet they would never allow you back in without a fight.

In that case, what would be the point of fighting Narváez with your full force? By leaving a strong contingent of soldiers in Tenochtitlán, you ensure that you can reenter the city and complete your plans to seize the empire's wealth. As long as they hold Moctezuma hostage and keep out of trouble, the men you leave behind should have no problems with the Aztec people while you are away.

Leaving soldiers in Tenochtitlán when you desperately need them against the larger forces of Narváez may seem foolish, but you do hold several advantages. Your soldiers have been battle tested in skirmishes with the Tlaxcalans. Narváez's force has not. You are familiar with the lay of the land. Narváez is not. Also, remember that many Spaniards have been lured to the New World by tales of gold. By displaying samples, you might be able to persuade Narváez's men to join you in skimming riches from the Aztecs. Furthermore, you may be able to recruit help from nearby expeditions by showing them the gold as well. Chances are, they have not had your luck in discovering wealth. This would give you a slightly larger army with which to face Narváez.

One possible problem with this plan is that you do not have a totally trustworthy commander to leave in charge at Tenochtitlán. Pedro de Alvarado is your second-in-command. While he has performed well in recent months, he nearly wrecked your expedition before it started. His was the first of your ships to land in Mexico. Immediately, he disobeyed your orders and began looting the natives' villages along the coast. His actions nearly cost you the friendship of the Tlaxcalans, whose help you will need if trouble starts between you and the Aztecs. You will have to hope that Alvarado has learned his lesson and will command sensibly.

Pedro de Alvarado (1485?-1541), your chief lieutenant, is your only choice if you leave someone behind in charge.

YOU ARE THE EXPLORER.
WHAT IS YOUR DECISION?

Option 1	Surrender yourself to Narváez.
Option 2	Flee with the gold.
Option 3	Lead your entire army against Narváez.
Option 4	Send part of your force to deal with Narváez.

Hernán Cortés (1485-1547) left Spain to make his name in the New World at the age of 19. He helped Diego Velázquez conquer Cuba, but their relationship was rocky even before Cortés's departure for Mexico.

Hernán Cortés chose *Option 4*.

Cortés was familiar with the history of political fighting among the Spanish in the New World. He had no faith that his conquests in Mexico and the gold that he acquired would help save him from Velázquez's anger. He also knew he could not count on officials in Spain defending him because of his newfound gold. So he had no intention of giving himself up to Narváez and risking imprisonment or death.

Cortés was also a gambler by nature. Like many Spaniards, he had come to the New World in search of fame and fortune. Although he had distinguished himself in the Spanish conquest of Cuba and received his rewards, Cortés was far from satisfied. He realized that this Mexican expedition was his only chance to satisfy his craving for wealth and power. His goal was to control the Aztec Empire. Therefore, he had no intention of running away, and he could not be satisfied with simply defeating Narváez. Whatever he did, the desire to acquire the wealth of the Aztecs was foremost in his mind. As long as he saw a chance of reaching his goal, no matter how slim, he was determined to go after it.

Cortés also had incredible confidence in his own abilities as a battle commander. Narváez had a force of 900 men. Yet Cortés did not hesitate to split his smaller army. Leaving all but 70 of his own troops behind in Tenochtitlán, he picked up another 260 men in reinforcements from two other nearby expeditions. Cortés set out to defeat Narváez's army with a force of just over one-third the size.

RESULT

Cortés marched his small army to meet Narváez's force near Vera Cruz, on the Mexican coast. Cortés ordered a few of his men to sneak into Narváez's camp, carrying gold pieces they had received from Moctezuma. They quietly spread the word that there was plenty more where this came from—enough for every soldier among them to return home a rich man. All they had to do was join Cortés, who knew how to get the gold.

The lure worked. Cortés launched a surprise attack at night, quickly capturing Narváez. Narváez's soldiers eagerly abandoned their leader. With his daring stroke, Cortés eliminated the threat from Narváez and greatly strengthened his army. With 900 fresh troops under his control, Cortés suddenly found himself in command of the largest European military force in the New World.

The other part of the operation, however, was a disaster. Pedro de Alvarado, whose only job was to avoid trouble until Cortés returned, botched his assignment. The preparations for a peaceful Aztec religious ceremony frightened him into thinking that the Aztecs were preparing to attack him. He panicked, sending his soldiers to break up the ceremony. In the process, they massacred many innocent Aztecs.

Alvarado's actions so enraged the Aztecs that they no longer cared whether these strangers were gods or not. Cortés returned to Tenochtitlán to find his men cowering behind barricades surrounded by hostile Aztecs.

Cortés tried to find a peaceful solution. He convinced Moctezuma to appeal to the Aztecs to calm down.

But the people were so angry at the Spanish that they considered Moctezuma's remarks treason. They shot arrows and threw stones at him, killing him and depriving Cortés of his insurance against attack. Suddenly, Cortés found himself holed up in the middle of a hostile city, surrounded by Aztec warriors. With their food and water cut

The Aztecs themselves killed their king, believing he was in league with the foreigners.

off and the Aztecs continuing to attack their headquarters, the Spanish were in a desperate situation.

The Spanish tried to escape with their gold under the cover of night, but the Aztecs detected them. Their attack cut Cortés's forces in two. Desperately fighting for his own survival, Cortés could not help the trapped soldiers. He finally staggered out of the city along with about 440 men and 20 horses. "It was a miracle any of us escaped," he wrote later. Nearly 600 of his men never made it out. Cortés also lost all of the gold he had received from the Aztecs, most of it falling into the lakes surrounding Tenochtitlán along with the Spanish who died trying to escape with it.

Although his hopes for an easy conquest of Mexico were shattered, Cortés refused to give up. In the early summer of 1521, Cortés led a powerful army of his remaining men, some gold-hungry Spanish reinforcements, and thousands of Tlaxcalans back to Tenochtitlán. He laid siege to the city, cutting off its water and food supplies. Unknown to him, however, the ultimate weapon of destruction lay in the germs his own soldiers inadvertently carried. A smallpox epidemic, introduced by the Spanish the last time they were in Tenochtitlán, swept through the city. With no natural resistance to this disease, the Aztecs died by the tens of thousands. By August 1521, the decimated Aztecs were too weak to resist any longer.

After nearly two years of effort, Cortés had finally taken control of the now destroyed city. The Spanish rebuilt it as Mexico City and made it their base of operations in the New World for the next 300 years.

ANALYSIS

Cortés's decision worked out well for him personally. Not only did he escape the clutches of Velázquez, but he also managed to achieve his goal of conquering the Aztec Empire. Had he surrendered to Narváez or tried to escape overland, he would have been lucky to survive and certainly would never have accomplished his goal.

On the other hand, his decision resulted in disaster for nearly everyone else involved. Leaving Alvarado in charge at Tenochtitlán was a terrible blunder that cost the lives of more than a thousand Spanish soldiers, thousands of Tlaxcalans, and well over a hundred thousand

An Aztec calendar stone. By eliminating the Aztecs and destroying Tenochtitlán, Cortés also destroyed a unique and inventive culture.

Aztecs. It also cost Cortés his goal of ruling over one of the wealthiest and most majestic empires in the world. By the time he took control of Tenochtitlán, the city was nothing but a burning rubble, reeking of death. The Aztecs were destroyed and the gold had been lost.

Cortés could hardly have done worse had he taken his entire command out of Tenochtitlán to deal with Narváez and then sought a way to return to the city. He would have lost his vantage point, but Pedro de Alvarado would not have angered the Aztecs. With Moctezuma still alive and under his command, Cortés could have used the Aztec king to place the Spanish back in Tenochtitlán. From there, he might have been able to conquer the empire and save the gold.

4

PASSAGE AROUND THE
AMERICAS
1520

There it is! At long last you have found the ocean passage around the American continent. If your calculations are correct, you will now be able to prove that it is possible to reach Asia by sailing west. King Charles I, the 19-year-old ruler of Spain who sponsored your voyage, will be thrilled to learn of this alternative ocean route to the valuable spice trade.

This should be a moment of great triumph, but instead it is a time of grave uncertainty. Your ships have been sailing under a cloud of bad luck. You have experienced a shipwreck, a freezing winter at the southern end of the South American coast, and a full-scale mutiny by your sailors. Recently, you have learned that you were

By discovering the strait, you overcame a giant hurdle in your journey to the Indies. But travel through the waterway could prove to be slow and difficult.

cheated on your supplies. The passage through the rocky strait that leads to the eastern ocean promises to be extremely difficult. You have no idea what awaits you on the other side once you do get through the strait.

How do you proceed?

BACKGROUND

You have the same problem that Christopher Columbus had—you are a foreign captain leading a Spanish expedition. Like Columbus, you had tried to persuade Portugal to finance a journey that you were certain would bring wealth for the nation. As a veteran of many wars and expeditions for Portugal, you expected its support. But the king refused to back you. The Portuguese are already using the African route to the Indies—the islands and mainland that make up parts of South, Southeast, and East Asia—pioneered by Vasco da Gama. Portugal has no desire to experiment with an uncertain western route.

Desperate for someone to sponsor your expedition, you turned to Spain.

That decision leaves you with few friends. As Spain is Portugal's enemy, the Portuguese consider you a traitor. But many of the Spanish sailors under your command do not trust you, either. Some believe you are a secret agent whose job is to destroy the Spanish expedition. Even before you left port, you received a letter from a friend warning you that three of your captains were planning to kill you!

Under these dangerous circumstances, you sailed from Spain on August 10, 1519, with five ships and approximately 280 crew men under your command. You expected to find either open ocean around the bottom of South America or a strait that would lead you through it. Your plan was to find this passage during the warmer summer months (November to March in the southern hemisphere). Unfortunately, the strait proved farther south than anyone expected. You spent months crawling along the coast in search of the passage. By the time winter arrived, you still had not found it.

Freezing weather and rough waters forced you to halt your search and wait out the winter. This caused you to use up a great deal more of your food supply than intended. During this time of miserable weather and boredom, sailors began to complain. They could see no point in going farther.

The captains who hate you took advantage of the discontent and started their long-planned mutiny. At one point, they captured three of your five ships and made plans to return to Spain. But with the help of loyal crew members, you regained the ships and put down the mutiny. You then ordered the death of one of the rebels and left two more marooned on the shore. About 40 of the crew men who supported the mutiny have spent the winter at hard labor in chains. Shortly after dealing with the mutiny, you discovered you had been greatly shorted of food. Bribed by Portuguese officials, your suppliers in Spain had badly skimped on the stores of biscuit, salted meats, and other foods that you ordered.

In the spring, you continued down the coast of South America, losing one of your ships to a storm. On October 21, 1520, according to the ship's historian, you finally stumbled upon the bay you were looking for. Two of your ships scouted the inlet and reported that it appears to be a deep, narrow stretch of water (known as a strait) through the land to open sea on the other side. But the strait winds through rocky terrain. There are so many bays and islands in the strait that you may have to spend

Shortly after discovering the strait, you realized just how difficult travel through the waterway to the Pacific Ocean would be.

many days picking your way through this maze to the other side.

No European has ever sailed in the waters on the far side of the Americas. If your calculations are correct, you should be able to cross that ocean in a matter of days to reach the Indies and its spices. But this is only a guess, and the actual distance could be much longer. You might even find more land lying in the way of your path to the Indies.

THE DECISION IS YOURS.

You are sailing with many crew members who have not been trustworthy. Supplies are tight. You are faced with a mysterious and dangerous strait. Beyond that lies an ocean of unknown size. What are your orders?

Option 1 **Divide your fleet and proceed into the strait.**

You made an agreement with the Spanish government to find and explore an all-water passage either through or around the Americas to the Indies. At this point, you don't have many friends in the world. Your only chance of gaining respect and fame is to complete this mission and win the gratitude of King Charles. He has promised you a share of the profits of this voyage plus the title of governor of all islands you discover. But if you return home empty-handed, your jealous enemies will probably succeed in turning Charles against you.

Perhaps the voyage has not gone as smoothly as you would have liked. But unexpected problems are a normal part of any expedition. If you wanted everything safe and secure, you would have stayed at home.

Food supplies may be lower than expected, but you are not out yet. Even those who want to return to Spain agree that you have about two months' worth of food on board. In addition, you can fish and hunt penguins and other birds to add to your supplies. Hopefully, you will be able to reach the Indies before all your food runs out.

But you have very little margin for error. To get through the strait as quickly as possible, you need to split up the fleet and explore as many bays as you can. You don't want to waste time by having all four ships sail into the same dead-end bays. You can move through the strait much more quickly by having each ship check out a certain number of bays and possible passages and then report back to the others.

Option 2 Proceed into the strait but keep the fleet together.

You need to keep going into the strait for reasons stated in **Option 1.** But even if splitting up your fleet to scout the strait would save time, you dare not risk it. This expedition is not one big happy family. Sailors already tried to mutiny once and came close to succeeding. Those who joined the mutiny may never forgive you for punishing their leaders. Several of your pilots do not like your chances of crossing the ocean. One of your most experienced pilots, Esteban Gomes, has made no secret of the fact that he thinks you are crazy to try and continue this voyage.

With this much opposition, you would be wise to keep all the ships together where you can keep an eye on them. Splitting up to scout the bays will tempt the crew members and captains who do not want to continue. Once they are out of your sight, they could take over their ship and head straight back for home.

Of course, staying together would slow your passage through the strait. That might make food supplies even tighter. But the sacrifice is necessary to keep the voyage together and going. Once everyone makes it to the Indies, no one will be complaining.

Option 3 **Return to Spain for fresh supplies and then make a second voyage.**

Your main task was to find the passage through or around the Americas. You are positive you have accomplished that mission. Therefore, even if you were to return to Spain now, you could do so with your head held high.

Finding the passage took a great deal longer than expected. That is not your fault. No one even knew for certain that a passage existed. But this delay has caused your expedition to run short of food. You would be foolish to risk all you have achieved by trying to finish the trip without enough supplies. After all, you do not really know how much ocean you have yet to cross before you reach the Indies. Esteban Gomes warns that "with provisions for a bare two months, it would be madness to head into the unknown."

Think of what you could lose by continuing. If your fleet were to die of starvation before reaching the Indies, your knowledge of the passage would be lost. Remember also that a hungry crew is an unhappy crew. Given the strained relationship between you and the crew members, you do not want to give them any reason to consider another mutiny.

You can still achieve your goal of sailing west to the Indies without taking that risk. All you have to do is return to Spain and load up on supplies. This time you know exactly where the passage is, so you won't have to waste months looking for it. You will be able to sail to the passage—and hopefully to the Indies— comfortably and with more supplies.

Now that you have found the strait, it should be easy to identify by the terrain that surrounds it (in case you want to leave it for now and return).

Option 4 Turn around and sail east to the Indies.

You really have two missions on this expedition. As mentioned, the first is to find a passage through the Americas to the Indies. Although you believe you have found that passage, what will you have to show for it? The second part of your mission is to bring back some of the wealth of the Indies. If you return to Spain with an empty ship, the expedition gains nothing financially. Given the distrust of you as a foreigner, you could be in big trouble with Spanish officials.

There is, however, one way to achieve success without returning home and without risking the unknown ocean with meager supplies. You could turn around now and sail *east* to the Indies. Some of your more experienced officers are urging you to do this. They know the distance to the Indies via the African route and are certain you can reach them with your present supplies. Then your ships can be loaded up with goods from the Indies. You could make a fortune for both yourself and Spain.

You would then return to Spain with both information about a passage through the Americas to the Indies and the riches you were sent to get. Mission accomplished. If you still felt bad about not completing your passage through the Americas, you could form another expedition in Spain. Or, since you know at about what latitude the passage exists, you could load up on supplies in the Indies and sail back to Spain through that American passage. That would give you a more secure food supply with which to venture into the unknown ocean.

Option 5 Load up two ships and send the rest back.

For reasons given in *Option 1*, you want to continue through the strait. But you have to be concerned about the low food supplies. You are only guessing how wide the far ocean is; you do not know for certain. The risk of sailing into that unknown expanse of water with limited food supplies is foolhardy.

You could solve both the problems of limited food and of disgruntled crew members in one easy step. Put most of the food supplies on the two largest vessels. Then send the other two ships back to Spain with just enough food for the voyage. You can get rid of all the trouble-makers by sending them in this group.

If you do this, however, you would be taking another risk by sailing into an unknown ocean with only two ships. There would be little assistance if you should run into any problems. Also, once you do reach the Indies, you would only have two ships to load up on spices to bring back to Spain. Returning with only a partial shipment of the spices you were expected to bring may not look good in the eyes of your sponsors.

YOU ARE THE EXPLORER. WHAT IS YOUR DECISION?

Option 1   **Divide your fleet and proceed into the strait.**

Option 2   **Proceed into the strait but keep the fleet together.**

Option 3   **Return to Spain for fresh supplies and then make a second voyage.**

Option 4   **Turn around and sail east to the Indies.**

Option 5   **Load up two ships and send the rest back.**

Ferdinand Magellan (1480-1521) loyally served the Portuguese military at sea for nine years. But he left Portugal for Spain after King Dom Manuel refused to grant him his request for a higher rank and to back his voyage to the Indies.

Ferdinand Magellan chose *Option 1*.

Magellan was determined to complete his mission. He suspected that his many enemies would be able to turn the king against him unless he accomplished exactly what he had promised. That meant plunging ahead with all of his ships, even if supplies were tight. According to one crew member, Magellan announced, "Even if we have to eat the leather wrappings on the masts and the yards, I will still go on to discover what I have promised."

Magellan believed that he had crushed the mutiny. He was aware that there were still a few grumblers like Gomes on board. But he did not think they would dare try anything after what had happened to the previous mutiny leaders. Therefore, he had no concerns about splitting up the fleet to scout the best route through the bewildering strait. That strategy would get them through the strait in the shortest amount of time.

RESULT

Magellan sent two ships to scout two possible passages through the strait. One of the ships returned from the mission; the other, the *San Antonio*, did not. Thinking that the ship had run into trouble, Magellan searched for it. He spent many days sailing back and forth along the strait before he gave up the search.

After 38 nerve-racking days maneuvering through the rocky strait, Magellan finally reached a wide, calm ocean. He named this water Mar Pacifico, or the Pacific Ocean, hoping it would remain as peaceful as he had found it. From there, he set sail for where he believed the Indies to be.

Unknown to Magellan, the *San Antonio*'s pilot, Esteban Gomes, had waited until he had sailed out of sight of the other ships and then led another mutiny. He succeeded in wresting control of the ship from Magellan's cousin. Then he sailed the ship back to Spain.

Losing the *San Antonio* was a severe blow for Magellan. It was the largest of the fleet's four remaining ships and held the most food. Now, with no margin for error, Magellan sailed into the Pacific, hoping to reach land before the food ran out. Unfortunately, the ocean turned out to be far wider than he had anticipated. His three-ship fleet sailed for almost two months without spotting land. The intense tropical heat quickly spoiled what little food remained. The desperate crew survived on rats, sawdust, and ox hide sail coverings. Six weeks into their journey from the strait, sailors began dying of starvation. Many more lay near death when they finally reached land on January 25, 1521. But this was not the islands they were hoping for. The crew set sail, and it would be over a month before they could land again. This time it was in the Philippines, just north of their destination and only days after they had used up the last of their food.

More tragedy awaited Magellan there. He unwisely got involved in a local tribal war on land and was killed on April 27, 1521. His crew continued the voyage, but it was never able to shed its string of bad luck. Two more ships were disabled; most of the crew members died of hunger, diseases, and wounds in battles with natives.

Magellan was killed with only a handful of loyal men fighting by his side. The rest were aboard the ships, waiting until after their Portuguese leader was dead to rescue the others.

On September 8, 1522, over three years after leaving Spain, the lone remaining ship, the *Victoria*, struggled back to port. Only 18 starving crew members of the original 280 survived the first voyage around the world.

The 90-ton Victoria *was the third largest of the original fleet's ships and the first ship to sail around the world.*

ANALYSIS

Like Columbus, Magellan made a serious miscalculation on the size of the earth. He believed that the Indies were not far from the Americas and, therefore, that he could survive on the food available.

He would have had more food had he not made the mistake of letting the *San Antonio* out of his sight. Had that ship not deserted, Magellan's crew would have faced a slightly better chance of surviving the long voyage across the Pacific. Gomes had made no secret of his strong opposition to continuing the voyage. So his take-over of the ship to steer it home should not have been a surprise. Furthermore, Magellan wasted valuable time searching for the *San Antonio* and did not emerge from the strait for more than five weeks.

Had Magellan kept all of his ships together, it is difficult to say how long it would have taken the fleet to get through the strait. But it would have been an advantage to have the largest ship holding the most food when the expedition spent over three months on the ocean, suffering from scurvy and starvation.

Magellan's decision subjected his crew to terrible agonies. "I think that never man will undertake to perform such a voyage," wrote Antonio Pigafetti, one of the crew members, recounting the horrors of starvation. He kept a daily account of the voyage.

Disastrous as it was, Magellan's decision would have turned out even worse had it not been for unusually good weather. The Pacific Ocean remained peaceful, and Magellan found favorable winds and currents. Magellan was lucky his entire expedition did not perish, never to be heard from again.

In the end, the voyage brought Magellan everlasting fame as the leader of the first expedition to sail around the world. And the strait he discovered near the southern tip of South America was named the Strait of Magellan. But neither he nor most of his crew survived to savor the honor. Also, the trip failed to achieve its main goal of pioneering a sensible trade route to the Indies through the Americas. Long before he died, Magellan realized that the distance across the Pacific Ocean was so great that the western route to the Indies was totally impractical.

5

IN THE CROSSFIRE
OF THE INDIAN WARS
1609

You have been placed in charge of France's new settlements of land in North America, known as New France. In addition to establishing a permanent town at Quebec, you have the task of exploring the vast forests on both sides of the St. Lawrence River to build a fur trade.

Like many explorers, you find native people living in the lands you wish to explore. Many of these inhabitants are suspicious of white newcomers and guard their territory cautiously. They are not afraid to take up arms and fight against strangers. Although their weapons are no match for European firepower, they far outnumber your tiny settlement. Their knowledge of the land and their

*A seventeenth-century musket may appear simple,
but it is weapons like these that give you an
advantage in the Canadian wilderness.*

skill in hand-to-hand fighting also make them dangerous.

Complicating the situation is the long history of
warfare between the various tribes. The many tribes in
the regions you wish to explore and settle are divided
into two main groups who are bitter enemies. If these
neighbors are hostile, it can make exploration extremely
dangerous. Somehow you must find a way to protect
your expeditions and settlement from Indian attacks.

BACKGROUND

One of your competitors in the New World, Spain, has
shown that the Americas can produce tremendous riches
for adventurous Europeans. Other countries are now
scrambling to grab as much of these new lands as they
can. France's main rival, Great Britain, is starting to
explore and establish settlements in the lands to the south
of New France. By exploring and settling the territory

around the St. Lawrence, you can make sure that France has a strong claim to this area.

France's first efforts to establish a settlement at Quebec in the 1530s and 1540s failed due to disease, hunger, cold weather, and lack of support from the government. The French abandoned the colony for more than half a century. This latest group of settlers arrived in 1608. Although this colony is stronger than past settlements, it remains a relatively weak and remote outpost. The French government has not been known to spend

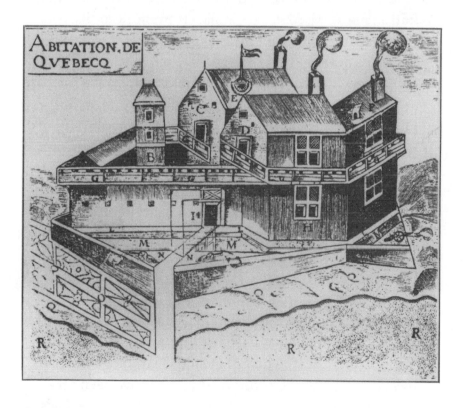

Shortly after arriving at Quebec, you built this fort for protection against attacks and the harsh winters.

lavishly on their explorations, and you can expect minimal help from them.

The woodlands around the St. Lawrence have become especially attractive because of the many animals there with valuable pelts. The money from the fur trade could provide the financing that your settlement needs to survive.

Many explorers, you included, are also convinced that a "northwest passage" through the continent exists near New France. The Indians' stories offer evidence that if you follow the St. Lawrence River west, you may find an all-water route to China. If France can discover this route, it could claim the passage as its own and gain a huge advantage in trade to the Far East.

Most of the lands to the west that you wish to explore are in territory controlled by tribes known as the Hurons and the Algonquins. Their enemies, a group of tribes known as the Iroquois League of Five Nations, hold the lands to the south and east. The clashes between these groups have been going on for longer than anyone can remember. Vicious wars and cruelty on both sides have made this an especially bitter conflict.

French settlers have had fairly good relations with the Huron and Algonquin tribes ever since Jacques Cartier first explored the St. Lawrence River some 70 years ago. But there has been occasional friction. These tribes are not keen on the idea of European invaders moving into the forests where they and their ancestors have lived for centuries. For this reason, they have been reluctant to cooperate with French plans to explore these lands, especially the lands richest in fur, which they use too.

Jacques Cartier (1491-1557) meeting and trading with Indians for the first time in 1535

At the same time, the Hurons and Algonquins have shown an interest in making an alliance with French settlers against the Iroquois. So far, the French have had very little contact with the Iroquois League. Another complication is that your bitter enemy, Great Britain, has begun exploring and settling along the Atlantic coast to the south of Quebec. If they start to move inland towards New France, they will be going through Iroquois territory and may look to trade and to form an alliance with them.

THE DECISION IS YOURS.

New France's furs provide a great opportunity for your tiny settlement to achieve massive wealth for both itself and France. But first you must address the long-standing rivalry the Hurons and Algonquins have with the Iroquois. What is your strategy for dealing with the Indians and ensuring your survival and success?

Option 1 **Form an alliance with the Hurons and Algonquins against the Iroquois.**

Despite your superior weapons, you do not have a powerful military force under your command at the moment. If history is any indication, you are not likely to get one any time soon. Unlike Spain, France has never spent the money to send large armies to conquer the inhabitants of the Americas.

That leaves you in an exposed position out in the northern forests. You cannot afford to be on bad terms with your closest Indian neighbors, the Hurons and Algonquins. This is especially true if you want to explore lands or obtain furs. In such dense forest areas, the only practical method of transportation over long distances is by river. The Algonquin and Huron Indians control virtually all the river passages to the north and west—the lands in which France has the greatest interest.

Since you need friends, and since friendship with the Hurons and Algonquins will offer you great advantages in exploration and fur trapping, an alliance with them makes sense. The one thing the Hurons and Algonquins want most from you is help in fighting their

The Hurons are an Iroquoian-speaking nation, even though they are enemies of the Iroquois League of Five Nations.

enemies. In fact, this is so important to them that they probably will not cooperate with you unless you agree to fight with them against the Iroquois.

Although you do not have many soldiers, your advanced weaponry will give you and your allies a decisive advantage over the Iroquois. With your allies gaining the upper hand in their long-standing war, your settlements and explorations should remain relatively free of danger from Indians. As an added bonus, they will push back the Iroquois and prevent Great Britain from establishing trade with them in this area.

Option 2 **Stay neutral in the Indian wars.**

While you may find a short-term advantage in allying with the Hurons and Algonquins, such an alliance would likely be a dangerous course of action. You are a stranger in these parts. You do not know the complete history of the warfare between the Indian groups; nor do you know much about the Iroquois. When you do not know what you are dealing with, the wisest course of action is to stay out of other people's disputes. Remember what happened to Ferdinand Magellan in the Philippines when he got involved with a tribal dispute that did not concern him? He got himself killed.

What if the Iroquois should turn out to be far more powerful than the Hurons and Algonquins? By making an alliance with their hated enemies, you could be earning the undying hostility of powerful and merciless people who otherwise might not have bothered you.

Morally, you have no business getting involved in this dispute. The Iroquois have done you no harm. You would be wrong to make war suddenly against people who have done nothing to deserve it, simply to get what you want.

Furthermore, you would be foolish to spend time and effort fighting someone else's battles. You need to concentrate on both exploration and establishing a prosperous settlement. While the Hurons and Algonquins may not like your neutrality, you might be able to survive without them. If you remain peaceful and friendly, eventually both they and the Iroquois will come to accept you as good neighbors and allow you to explore and trap in the woodlands without the fear of attack.

*An Iroquois warrior. The Iroquois League of Five
Nations consists of the Mohawk, Oneida, Onondaga,
Cayuga, and Seneca tribes.*

Option 3 **Support the Hurons and Algonquins against the Iroquois but do not actually fight.**

The dispute between the Hurons and Algonquins and the Iroquois is so heated that you cannot remain neutral. Neither side will consider you a friend if you refuse to help them in their life-and-death struggle with their enemy. They will only see you as a weak third party trying to steal their land and furs. But while you need the cooperation of the Hurons and Algonquins, you do not want to upset the Iroquois.

This leaves you in a ticklish situation that calls for a delicate strategy. Somehow you must offer enough support to satisfy the Hurons and Algonquins that you are their friends but not enough to make the Iroquois turn into your enemies. The best way to do this is to offer weapons, training, and medical care to the Hurons and Algonquins but to stay out of any actual fighting.

This kind of help may benefit your allies so much that they will reward you by cooperating in your exploration and fur-trapping ventures. By choosing this option, you accomplish your objectives without risking loss of life either now or in the future.

Option 4 **Secretly offer help to both sides and later choose the stronger ally.**

You are caught in a no-win situation. Unless you fight with the Hurons and Algonquins, they are not likely to cooperate with you. Their struggle with the Iroquois is so intense that they will offer their friendship only to those willing to take up war against their enemies. They will scoff at you for remaining neutral or avoiding conflict and will consider you cowardly. On the other hand, if you do fight, you will provoke the Iroquois into being your enemies for life.

Since there is no good way to gain the favor of both sides, you are better off trying to limit their effectiveness as possible enemies. If you can keep the two groups focused on fighting each other, they will pay less attention to you. Even better, they will eventually weaken each other to the point where they no longer present as great a threat to your ventures.

You can accomplish this by selling weapons to both sides and by secretly stirring up trouble between the two groups as often as possible. If one group begins to take a decisive advantage in the war, then you know it is the stronger of the two. You can then join forces with that group to finish off the other.

YOU ARE THE EXPLORER.
WHAT IS YOUR DECISION?

Option 1   **Form an alliance with the Hurons and Algonquins against the Iroquois.**

Option 2   **Stay neutral in the Indian wars.**

Option 3   **Support the Hurons and Algonquins against the Iroquois but do not actually fight.**

Option 4   **Secretly offer help to both sides and later choose the stronger ally.**

*Samuel de Champlain (1567-1635) made his first
trip to the New World as part of a Spanish fleet to the
West Indies, Mexico, and Panama. From this
experience, he learned of the enormous value the New
World potentially held for his own country, France.*

Samuel de Champlain chose *Option 1*.

The French usually tended to deal more humanely with the people they encountered in the Americas than did their European rivals. Champlain, a court geographer and son of a sailor, was also of a more peaceful nature than most of the Spanish and Portuguese explorers. Yet he saw the fur trade and exploration of the forests around the St. Lawrence River as crucial to the survival of the colony that was entrusted to his command.

The settlement knew its immediate problem was the opposition of the Hurons and Algonquins to French

From the very beginning, Champlain knew the success of his colony would depend on his trade with his closest neighbors, the Hurons and Algonquins.

exploration and trade. The only way to solve it was to win the gratitude of these people by joining them in war against their bitter enemies.

Champlain had been one of the few foreigners whom Spain had allowed to travel along with its expeditions to the New World. From this, he was aware of the huge military advantage European weapons provided. He had also learned the importance of making alliances with Indians. Champlain reasoned that a few displays of force against the Iroquois would demonstrate enough superiority to satisfy the Hurons and Algonquins and discourage the Iroquois from continuing the war. After that, Champlain planned to have "the heathen . . . converted and a passage discovered to the East."

Therefore, before setting out on an exploration of lands in 1609, Champlain made a deal with the Hurons and Algonquins. If they would serve as guides, he would agree to join them in a battle with the Iroquois.

RESULT

While traveling south and west with several hundred Indian allies in 1609, Samuel de Champlain and two other colonists became the first Europeans to explore the Green Mountains of present-day Vermont and the Adirondack Mountains of what is now upstate New York. On the southern shore of a large lake that Champlain named for himself, the group came upon a party of Mohawks, who were part of the Iroquois League of Five Nations.

After a night of "dancing and singing on both sides" and "endless insults," the enemies formed for battle in the morning. Champlain stepped in front of his Indian allies and aimed his gun at those whom his allies identified as chiefs. He fired and killed two of them instantly and mortally wounded a third. Having never seen firearms before, the Iroquois were terrified by the explosion and the lethal effect. They fled into the woods.

For the next several years, the French enjoyed an excellent working relationship with the Hurons and Algonquins. The French and their allies set up a fur-trapping and trading system that extended all the way west to Lake Huron. The French settlement sold furs at a handsome profit to European buyers.

The battle at Lake Champlain, as illustrated by Champlain. Two inaccuracies of note in the picture: the Indians were always clothed, and palm trees are not native to the region.

But the Iroquois, infuriated by the Huron and Algonquin successes, stepped up their attacks. By 1615, Champlain's Indian allies were no longer bringing in the furs that had helped finance the colony. They complained that the Iroquois had grown more bold in their war. Iroquois attacks made it nearly impossible to carry furs along the rivers back to Quebec. Again, the Hurons and Algonquins offered to show Champlain new lands if he would join them in a campaign against the Iroquois.

Champlain organized a major attack. The Indians and French, however, could not coordinate their assault. Champlain was wounded and spent the next winter hiding among the Hurons, while the Iroquois remained strong.

Champlain's allies repaid his efforts by helping him explore lands around Lake Ontario and Lake Huron. But the explorer's hope that these lakes provided a passage through the American continent proved futile.

Meanwhile, the Iroquois grew stronger and more determined to conquer their enemies. They unleashed an ongoing campaign of annihilation against the Hurons. As one Frenchman noted in despair, "[The Iroquois] gain every year from our losses. They crush our allies and make Iroquois of them." The Iroquois all but destroyed the Hurons as a people.

The collapse of the Hurons and the retreat of their allies, including the Algonquins, left the French unprotected in the wilderness. French trappers could no longer canoe the rivers without fear of an Iroquois attack. Farmers could not tend their fields, and those in the settlements could not even go to fetch water from the well without fear of an Iroquois ambush.

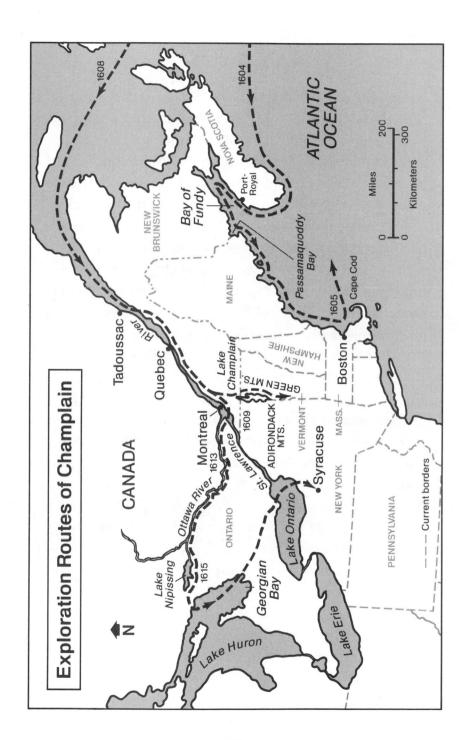

Exploration Routes of Champlain

CANADA

Lake Nipissing
1615
Ottawa River
1613
Lake Huron
Georgian Bay
Lake Erie
Lake Ontario
ONTARIO
St. Lawrence
Montreal
Syracuse
NEW YORK
ADIRONDACK MTS.
1609
VERMONT
PENNSYLVANIA
MASS.
NEW HAMPSHIRE
GREEN MTS.
Lake Champlain
Quebec
Tadoussac
River
MAINE
NEW BRUNSWICK
NOVA SCOTIA
Bay of Fundy
Port-Royal
Passamaquoddy Bay
Cape Cod
Boston
1605
1604
1608

ATLANTIC OCEAN

Miles
0   200
Kilometers
0   300

Current borders

N

ANALYSIS

In the short term, Champlain's alliance with the Huron and Algonquin tribes was probably his best choice for establishing a French colony in the Americas. Had he not agreed to join his closest neighbors, exploration would have been difficult, and the settlement would not have enjoyed the desperately needed profits of the fur trade.

If either the Hurons and Algonquins or the Iroquois had attacked his colony, it would have left Champlain with little protection. Since the French government was unwilling to offer much military support to the tiny settlement, Champlain and the settlers needed to obtain allies immediately. The only way to get the Hurons and Algonquins to comply was to join them in battle.

But, in the long term, the alliance helped doom France's dreams of a thriving New France. Champlain underestimated the strength of the Iroquois League of Five Nations, which happened to be one of the strongest alliances in North America. By meddling in a dispute that did not concern him, Champlain created an enemy that caused nothing but misery for his and other French settlements. The relentless attacks of the Iroquois badly weakened the French.

Champlain's alliance with the losing side also gave France's main rival a strong ally in North America. Great Britain benefited from Iroquois hatred of the French. It helped them gain the friendship of the Iroquois. Even after Champlain's death in 1629, the Iroquois never forgave New France for its earlier actions, and their hatred and attacks continued for decades.

6

STRANDED IN THE
MIDDLE OF NOWHERE
1770

Great Britain has assigned you the task of exploring the south Pacific Ocean. You have been sailing seas that no one from Europe has ever seen before as you map the coast of eastern Australia.

The thrill of discovery, however, has given way to an exhausting battle of nerves. For hundreds of miles, you have been nervously picking your way through a huge, deadly coral reef that lies off the coast of the continent. You are in constant danger of running aground on the sharp edges of the coral. There is no way to avoid the reef and still keep in sight of the land you are to chart.

While sailing late at night in the moonlight, your crew has been frequently measuring the depth of the

Recently, while sailing between the Great Barrier Reef and the coast, you passed by this group of islands, which you named the Whitsunday Islands. They lie about 400 miles southeast of your current position.

water to keep from running aground. On this evening, the coral has been down at a safe depth for quite some time. Suddenly, though, you hear a long grinding sound. Your ship, the *Endeavor*, slows and then stops altogether.

A captain's worst fears have come to pass. Your only ship is stuck on a coral reef thousands of miles from help.

BACKGROUND

This voyage is extremely important to Great Britain. For centuries, sailors have told tales of a rich continent and lush islands in the far south Pacific. Great Britain would like to learn if these tales are true. If the British could reach these new lands ahead of the rest of Europe, they could claim them as their own property.

Your long journey has established that there is no great continent in the South Pacific that extends all the way to the South Pole. Or if there is, it is so far south and so cold and icy that it would be worthless to your country.

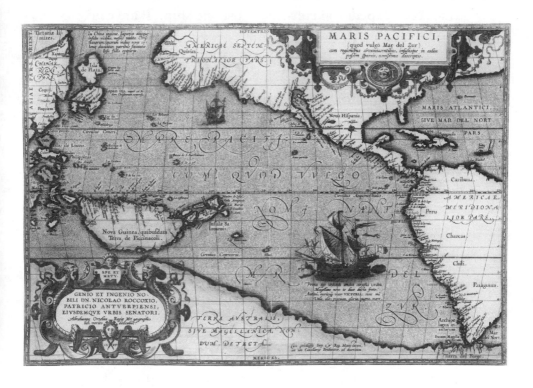

Geographers used to believe in the existence of a great southern continent, shown here at the bottom of this 1589 map of the Pacific Ocean and surrounding area. This continent would offset the larger landmasses of the northern hemisphere and balance the world.

But you have mapped the small continent of Australia and the islands of New Zealand, which Europeans know very little about. You have also found many other islands that would interest the British. At the moment, however, Great Britain has no idea as to what you have found. For the past couple of years, you have been so far from Europe that you have been unable to send any messages back home.

This puts you in a terrifying position, especially since your expedition consists of a single ship. If anything should happen to this ship, you have virtually no chance of returning home. No one in Great Britain knows where you are or where to begin searching the millions of square miles of ocean into which you have disappeared.

None of your sailors have had any experience with the incredible coral reef that you have struck. But you do know that it is sharp enough to cut through or punch holes into the bottom of your ship. In fact, as day broke the next morning, you could see splinters of wood from the ship's hull floating away on the waves.

There is worse news. The next morning's daylight also revealed the fact that you are currently a good 25 miles from shore. Furthermore, your measurements indicated that you struck the reef at the night high tide. In other words, you got stuck when the water level was the highest it gets at night. During the hours since, the water level had gone down. Even though you had lightened the ship by tossing away unneeded equipment, this was not enough when the daytime high tide came along. You have a number of small lifeboats on board, but not nearly enough to carry the whole crew to shore in one trip.

There are a few bits of hope to which you can cling. You were sailing very slowly and cautiously when you struck the reef. That should limit the damage to the ship's bottom from the coral. The sea is calm today, which means the ship is resting on the coral and not being ground against it by wind and waves. Observations show that you are lodged on a fairly narrow ridge of coral. The depth drops quickly on all sides. You were fortunate to have chosen a flat-bottomed ship for this voyage. Had you been sailing in a ship with the usual sloped bottom,

Your ship, the Endeavor, *was once used for transporting coal. It has a flat bottom and large storage area for your voyage's supplies.*

you probably would have tipped over by now. Finally, many sailors believe that night tides rise higher than day tides. Although the lightened *Endeavor* has now remained stuck during the daytime high tide, measurements show that this tide was several feet lower than the night tide. It could be that the *Endeavor* is light enough to float off during the higher night tide.

THE DECISION IS YOURS.

Despite the calm weather, your ship's bottom is being severely damaged. Water is leaking into the *Endeavor* at an alarming rate. Your men have been up all night and day taking turns pumping the water back out. What can you do to salvage the situation?

Option 1 **Sit tight; count on the night high tide to float the *Endeavor* off.**

Your chances of survival in an emergency are best if you remain calm. It takes a great deal of nerve to sit tight and wait for the tide, especially while water is leaking into the ship through its disintegrating bottom. But that is precisely the kind of nerve a good captain needs to show to a jittery crew.

Face the facts: If you lose the *Endeavor*, you probably will never see home again. Your family, friends, and government have no idea where you are or where to begin looking for you. The Pacific Ocean in which you have been sailing is so vast that Great Britain could mount expensive expeditions for the next half century and never find a trace of you.

Even if you managed to ferry your entire crew to shore, your chances of survival are slim. You would have a limited supply of weapons and ammunition with which to defend yourselves against any hostile natives. Without your food stores, you would be forced to live strictly off the land. Your ventures onto land have found a largely barren wilderness with few plants and little water. You would be lucky to find shelter from winds and rain.

Nor would there be any chance of leaving this land. You haven't seen trees sturdy enough to supply lumber for rebuilding an entire ship, which is almost beside the point since you do not have the tools for this. Imagine having to spend the rest of your lives starving, thirsty, dirty, and wearing rags for clothing. You would spend the remainder of your days in constant fear of attack from natives.

In other words, you have nothing to lose by staying with the ship. So focus all your efforts on saving your lifeline to the world. You have three pumps to empty water from the ship's hold. Keep the crew busy at those pumps.

The *Endeavor* was traveling very slowly when it ran aground, so it cannot be too firmly stuck. You must not take any rash actions. Although it is tempting to try and pull the ship off the coral, this could destroy the ship's bottom.

Just remain calm and hope the ship floats high enough in the night tide to float off the reef.

Option 2 **Pull the ship off the coral at night high tide.**

For reasons presented in *Option 1*, you need to stay with the *Endeavor*. But you would be foolish simply to do nothing and hope that the extra few feet of tide floats you off the coral. You cannot afford to stay stuck on this reef, and that means you must do everything in your power to get the ship off.

Sailors do have a method of pulling a stranded ship off a rock that would probably work for coral as well. You can throw out anchors into the ocean ahead of the ship (or behind if you choose to go that direction). When the anchors are firmly lodged, you pull on the ropes and slide the ship off its perch into deeper water.

There is a major risk with this option. Coral is made up of a very hard, rough material in odd shapes

Coral from the Great Barrier Reef. Coral, though beautiful, can prove deadly as a hazard to sailors.

The Great Barrier Reef at low tide

that can have many sharp edges. Dragging a ship across a stretch of coral could completely rip out the bottom. That could destroy your ship and leave you stranded.

Unfortunately, that is a risk you will have to take. The ship stayed firmly grounded during the daytime high tide and could well be lodged so soundly that it will remain stuck at nighttime high tide.

Your most urgent task is to free the ship from the reef. Land lies only 25 miles away. Even if you puncture the bottom in the process of pulling the ship off the coral, you might still be able to keep the ship afloat long enough with your pumps to reach shore. Once there, you could make the repairs needed to continue on your way.

Option 3 Ferry men to land now in your lifeboats; salvage what you can.

This is a situation that calls for decisive action. The *Endeavor* is stuck. From what you have seen of the tides and the position of the ship on the coral, there is no reason to believe the ship will float off on its own. Because of the leaks and the nature of the coral, it is not likely that you can move the ship safely off the reef without ripping out the bottom. Water would gush in, and the ship would sink like a rock.

Then what would you do? Every sailor aboard knows that once a ship goes down, the captain loses control of the crew. It would be every man for himself. Given the fact that you do not have enough boats to take everyone to land in one trip, this would result in a horrifying spectacle. Men would be scratching and clawing, even killing, each other to get one of those precious spots in the boat. Your expedition would be lost in the coral reef. All of your maps, scientific data, and other notes of discovery would be gone.

As captain of this expedition, you cannot let that happen. Your only chance of preserving order and dignity is to start the evacuation now, before the situation becomes critical. The seas are calm, and no storm clouds are in sight. There is a chance that you can ferry the crew to land in several shifts before the weather turns bad or the stranded ship falls apart.

You do not have to be so pessimistic about your chances of survival in Australia. People have been known to accomplish remarkable things when their survival depends upon it. Your crew could adapt quite well to the bleak surroundings.

Furthermore, rescue is not entirely out of the question. You would be situated on the coast of a major chunk of land. The European nations still believe in the great

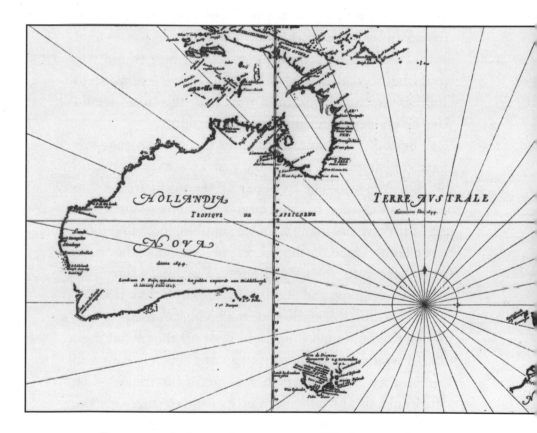

Europeans do know that some sort of land mass exists in the south Pacific Ocean, as this map from 1666 of the western portion of Australia shows.

southern continent and will surely not leave this part of the world unexplored. You hopefully would be able to spot any ship that sails along the eastern coast of Australia.

Option 4 **Break up the ship and build rafts.**

For reasons stated in **Option 3**, you need to begin evacuation now to avoid a sickening scramble for survival once the *Endeavor* goes down. But 25 miles is a long way to row small boats in the ocean. Since you have a shortage of space on those boats, some men would then have to row 25 miles back to the ship to get those left behind and then another 25 back to land. Another round trip would be needed if you still could not get everyone to land. If the weather should turn bad, the boats would have no chance of getting back to the ship.

Besides, the limited space on the boats means less space for supplies. That would make survival on land difficult. You would be far better off tearing apart the ship and using the wood to build large rafts. These rafts could carry the crew and many valuable supplies, including food, to the land. Once on the shore, you could use the wood from these rafts to build shelter to protect yourselves from the elements and possible attacks by native people.

Choosing this option means giving up the possibility that the lightened ship could float off the reef at high tide. It would also mean tearing apart a severely damaged ship you are still on, which may get a bit tricky. The rafts would also be difficult to propel and to steer over the 25 miles to land. But at least you could get everyone off the ship at the same time and heading toward land with a better chance of survival.

YOU ARE THE EXPLORER.
WHAT IS YOUR DECISION?

Option 1   Sit tight; count on the night high tide to float the *Endeavor* off.

Option 2   Pull the ship off the coral at night high tide.

Option 3   Ferry men to land now in your lifeboats; salvage what you can.

Option 4   Break up the ship and build rafts.

The son of a farmer, James Cook (1728-1779) would become one of the greatest explorers of all time. He set new standards in exploration for his clean ships, crew survival rate, thorough observations, and precise maps.

James Cook chose *Option 2*.

Cook did not view *Option 3* as reasonable. "We well knew that our boats were not capable of carrying us all on shore," he wrote. Cook was so pessimistic about the chances of surviving in that desolate wilderness and of the chances of getting rescued that he went on to say that any sailors left behind to drown on the sinking ship would "suffer less upon the whole than those who get to shore." Trying to build rafts out of the *Endeavor* would probably have proved to be too difficult and very time consuming. Therefore, *Option 4* never even crossed his mind.

But Captain Cook's other two options did not look so bright either. He realized that if the ship was leaking while lodged on the coral reef, then its bottom was already in bad shape. He suspected that the *Endeavor* was so badly damaged that getting off the reef "would probably precipitate our destruction." Trying to drag the ship off the coral would only make matters worse. But Cook was convinced the ship would not float off the reef by itself at night tide.

Based on that gloomy opinion, Cook saw no choice but to attempt to pull the ship off the reef and hope for a miracle. He knew he was gambling all of the men's lives on the fate of the *Endeavor*. Cook's only hope was that the crippled ship could make it to shore before it sank.

RESULT

Under their captain's calm leadership, the crew of the *Endeavor* waited for the night high tide that would either save or doom them. The crew members took turns operating the ship's three working pumps in exhausting shifts all through the day and into the night in a desperate attempt to hold back the water. But the leaks grew worse. Occasionally, a swell of the waves would slosh up against the ship. The men winced as they heard the grinding of the ship's wooden bottom against the coral. Fortunately, though, the calm weather held, and the crew continued to work and wait.

At high tide, the sea level rose enough for the crew to throw the anchors out into the water and pull the *Endeavor* off the reef. To Cook's immense relief, the ship did not immediately plunge to the bottom. But by this time, despite the furious efforts of the crew working the pumps, there was nearly four feet of water in the bottom of the ship. The *Endeavor* was sinking.

At this point, one of Cook's crew members suggested a technique, known as fothering, that he had seen tried on a previous voyage. Although unfamiliar with the technique, the captain ordered his crew to put it into action. The crew took a sail and smeared it with dung from sheep they had carried aboard as food. Several crew members swam down into the water and placed the sail against the leak underneath the boat. The pressure of the water rushing into the leak pressed the sail into the hole. Once it was in place, the film of sheep dung sealed the opening from further leakage.

This patchwork solution enabled the damaged *Endeavor* to reach the Australian shore. There the crew was able to repair the ship. They sailed off again shortly thereafter.

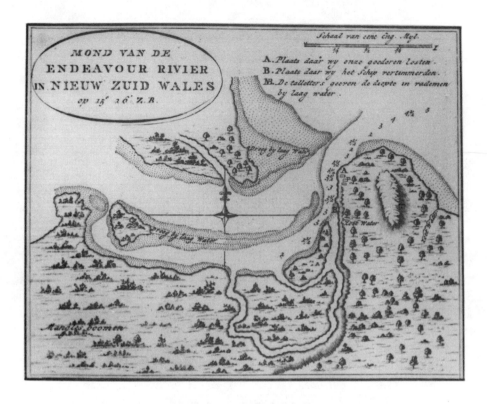

James Cook's map of the Endeavor River, where the expedition landed its ship for repairs

ANALYSIS

Since no one on board knew anything about coral reefs, Cook had to go entirely on instinct. He took a huge risk in choosing his course of action. In fact, had it not been for a stroke of luck, the *Endeavor* would have sunk as soon as it slid off the coral reef. When the men examined the ship while repairing it, they discovered a chunk of coral stuck in a gaping hole in the ship's hull. The coral had effectively plugged the hole that it had punched into the ship!

Once safely landed in the Endeavor River, the Endeavor *was tilted on one side, then the other, to repair its bottom.*

As it was, only a captain with tremendous leadership skills could have kept the crew on task at the pumps, preventing panic in the face of likely disaster.

One can only speculate as to what would have happened had Cook chosen to abandon ship and get his crew to shore. But it is certain that even had they been able to survive, they would not have been rescued for a long time—if at all. No ship passed this location for 30 years, and that was with the knowledge of the south Pacific Ocean that Cook's voyage provided. Had James Cook abandoned the *Endeavor*, the British would have known little of the South Pacific and might never have laid claim to such lands as Australia and New Zealand.

7

THE FORK IN THE RIVER
1805

You have been sailing upriver for months on a special mission for the President of the United States, Thomas Jefferson. Your task is to explore the western American wilderness, following the Missouri River to the Rocky Mountains and on to the Pacific Ocean.

Large rivers like the Missouri are a lifeline in an unmapped wilderness—you cannot get lost as long as you stay with the river. But as you set up camp at dusk on June 2 and look upstream, you get a knot in the pit of your stomach. There is a fork in the river.

The next morning, you study the two branches of the river and determine that either could be the Missouri. Indian scouts have given you important information about where to go and what to expect further upstream on the river. But that information is useless unless you can figure out which of these waterways is the Missouri. None of the scouting reports mentioned anything about a fork in this location. If you choose the wrong branch to lead you into the mountains, you could end up lost there with little chance of completing your mission.

BACKGROUND

President Jefferson set up this expedition several years ago when France still claimed ownership of most of these

Thomas Jefferson (1743-1826) has big plans for the Louisiana Territory. At first, it will be made into a giant reservation for Indians pushed off their lands east of the Mississippi River. Then Americans will begin settling it, moving the Indians farther west.

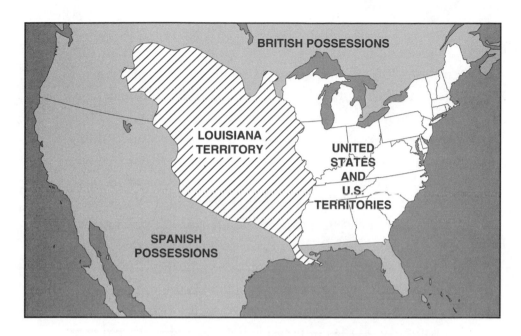

The Louisiana Purchase has doubled the size of the United States. With both Great Britain and Spain neighboring the territory, it is important to begin exploring and settling this land immediately.

western lands. Just before you began the trip, France sold this land, called the Louisiana Territory, to the United States for a bargain price. That makes it even more important that you find out exactly what the United States owns. Your other main objective is to determine trading possibilities in this region. Jefferson wants to know if there is an easily traveled water route to the Pacific Ocean. You also need to learn if the Indians in these lands are open to trade.

There are indications that the passage to the Pacific Ocean will not be too tough, even though Indian reports describe rugged mountains in the region. Alexander Mackenzie crossed the mountains in Canada about 400 miles north of your planned route while exploring for Great Britain a few years back. According to Mackenzie, the mountains he encountered were only about 3,000 feet high and posed no difficulty to travel. If the mountains are similar along your route, the journey should not be too difficult. Also, you know from sailors who have explored the Pacific Coast that the mighty Columbia River flows west into the Pacific Ocean. All you need to do is follow the Missouri River to the mountains, find a passage through those mountains, and then locate the Columbia River, which will take you to the ocean.

That is not to say the expedition has been a leisurely stroll through the countryside for you and the two dozen people who accompany you. For one thing, you are traveling with a very small force in Indian territory. You do not know what to expect from the various tribes. Already you had a near disaster with the Sioux on the lower Missouri River. They were insulted by the insufficient gifts you presented to win their friendship. This does not bode well for your current situation. Now you are moving through territory where the Assiniboin and Blackfeet tribes frequently roam. Both tribes are known to be hostile towards Americans and Europeans.

One of your most critical concerns is supplies. That was not a great problem as long as you were sailing up the Missouri with your large keelboat, stuffed with goods. But recently, you sent this boat back downstream because the Missouri now was becoming too swift and shallow for it. Also, you have been short of food on this trip.

You and your men greet the Mandans. If it weren't for the Mandans' hospitality, your expedition might have perished during the harsh winter.

You would have starved over the winter had the Mandan Indians not given you corn. More recently, an Indian guide named Sacagawea has had to help you out by showing you how to gather edible roots.

When you get farther upriver and into the mountains, you will have to abandon your boats, and maybe even several of your canoes. The only supplies you can take at this point are those that you can haul over land. Therefore, you will need to find the Shoshone Indians, sometimes known as the Snakes, who live there and trade with them for horses. As you wrote in your report to the president, "The Snake Indians possessing large quantities of horses is much in our favor, as by means of horses, the transportation . . . will be rendered easy and expeditious overland, from the Missouri, to the Columbia."

You have reason to believe that you have a good chance of trading with the Shoshones. There are several neighboring tribes that they wage war with, namely the Hidatsa and Blackfeet. These Indian tribes have been able to get firearms from European traders. This could make the Shoshones easy pickings for their enemies, if the Shoshones have no guns of their own. Given this scenario, the Shoshones would be eager for a new trading

You first met your fifteen-year-old guide, Sacagawea, in the Mandan villages. She joined your expedition and has been traveling with her newborn child.

partner and possible ally—the United States. Besides, your guide, Sacagawea, is a Shoshone who was kidnapped from her people by other Indians several years ago. She will help you in your trade relations with them.

In order to reach the Shoshones, however, you must follow the Missouri River into the mountains. That brings you back to the problem of which of these two branches is the Missouri. The Hidatsa Indians said that the next landmark along the way would be a great waterfall as the river comes out of the mountains. You have not seen the great falls, and the Hidatsas told nothing about this fork in the river.

The northern fork of the river comes straight out of the west; the southern fork flows from the southwest.

Hoping to find some clues as to which route to take, you have sent two scouting parties a short way up the rivers. They have come back with this information:

Sergeant Nathaniel Pryor reports that after about 10 miles, the northern branch turns to the north. Sergeant Patrick Gass did not travel quite as far on the southern branch. He reports that as of 6-1/2 miles, this branch of the fork continues to flow from the southwest. A second pair of scouting expeditions sent indicate that the rivers appear to flow from these directions for quite some distance.

The northern fork is about 200 yards wide and looks very similar to the river on which you have traveled. It flows slowly, but is a cloudy brown color from being full of mud. The surface is choppy with lots of ripples. The southern fork looks somewhat different from the lower Missouri. It is about 370 yards wide, but it is shallower.

The water is so clear and still that you can see the smooth stones resting on the river bottom.

Since this decision is so critical to the success of the expedition, all the men have been discussing and debating the issue. The man with the most experience traveling the Missouri River is Private Peter Cruzatte. He recommends taking the northern fork. His opinion carries a great deal of weight among the men, who agree that the northern branch is probably the Missouri River.

THE DECISION IS YOURS.

It is crucial that you find the Shoshones and cross the mountains before winter sets in. One of these two branches is the Missouri and will lead you to them. How do you determine which branch of the river is correct?

Option 1 Split the expedition in two and follow both rivers.

This decision is so critical to the expedition that you cannot afford to be wrong. Yet you do not have good information on which to base a decision. Therefore, the only way to ensure that at least some of your party reaches its destination is to split up and follow both routes.

This option gives you a great deal of flexibility. If one group quickly determines that its river is not the Missouri, it can double back and rejoin the other. If it takes several weeks before that group determines it is on the wrong river, it can simply turn around and go home.

Splitting your already small party in the middle of hostile Indian territory is dangerous. But everyone on your expedition knew the dangers involved in this journey when they agreed to come. The most important thing is for the mission to the Pacific to succeed, and you are obligated to take whatever risks necessary to accomplish that mission.

Option 2 **Follow the northern branch of the river.**

Splitting your expedition at this time and in this dangerous territory is a foolhardy risk. Moreover, it

A view of the northern branch of the fork in the river at sunset, one-half mile upstream from the fork

would demonstrate a lack of leadership. Making tough decisions is your job, so start making them.

Private Cruzatte is the man with the most experience on the Missouri River. You would be wise to listen to him. His opinion is based on facts that are plainly visible. You have been traveling on the Missouri for over a thousand miles. During that entire time, the river has never been anything but slow flowing and muddy. When in doubt, it is safer to assume that things will remain as they have been. Why would the river be suddenly starkly different? The muddy, turbulent northern branch looks exactly like the river on which you have traveled so far. The clear, fast-running southern branch looks entirely different.

Option 3 Follow the southern branch of the river.

For reasons stated above, you need to stay together and demonstrate good leadership by making a decisive choice.

But you should ignore Private Cruzatte and take the southern branch. While Cruzatte is experienced with the lower Missouri River, he has never traveled this far on the upper Missouri. He knows no more about this part of the river than anyone else on the expedition. And why should the upper Missouri look like the lower Missouri? The lower Missouri runs across a huge plain. No wonder the current runs slowly and the water is muddy. But now you are trying to reach the point at which the Missouri comes out of the mountains. A mountain river is naturally going to be clearer and swifter running than one going through plains.

Your co-captain of the expedition, William Clark (1770-1838), tends to feel the southern branch of the fork is correct. Clark was the commander of your company when you were in the army.

Option 4 **Send a small expedition up one of the rivers while the rest of the expedition waits.**

You cannot afford to be wrong. Yet you do not want to risk permanently splitting up your expedition. The best way to stay together and still ensure that you are on the right river is to take a week or two to send an expedition up one river.

You can do this with confidence because of a landmark that the Indians told you about—the great falls. According to their information, you should be running into those falls very soon. If you send a group of men upriver they will soon know if it is the correct choice by whether they find those falls or not. If they don't see the falls within a week or two, you can assume that this branch is not the Missouri River.

There is no sense in sending expeditions up both rivers because the one expedition is all you need to find whether the falls are on that river. If the falls are there, you have the right river. If the falls are not, the other is correct. Either way, your party is united and traveling on the Missouri River with a delay of at most several weeks.

There is one gnawing concern, however, with this decision. The Indians who told you about the falls neglected to tell you about this major fork in the river. If they could make such a glaring mistake about one landmark, how can you trust their information about these great falls to be accurate? You could waste time sending

During your journey, you have depended upon your councils with the various Indian tribes to provide you with what to expect farther along the river. Up to this point, the information has been correct.

an expedition to look for falls that don't exist. Then, when you don't find them, you might wrongly assume that the other route was the correct one. By that time, your expedition would be hopelessly confused, and your dwindling supplies would be gone. Even if you survived, you would never complete your mission.

YOU ARE THE EXPLORER.
WHAT IS YOUR DECISION?

Option 1   **Split the expedition in two and follow both rivers.**

Option 2   **Follow the northern branch of the river.**

Option 3   **Follow the southern branch of the river.**

Option 4   **Send a small expedition up one of the rivers while the rest of the expedition waits.**

Meriwether Lewis (1774-1809) became the head of a family plantation in Virginia at the age of 18. But he had always dreamed of becoming an explorer.

Meriwether Lewis chose *Option 3*.

After studying the two rivers, Captain Lewis concluded that the southern fork was like most rivers flowing from mountainous country. The fact that the northern branch was muddy indicated to him that it ran a great distance through a plain. Since he was expecting the Missouri River to lead him to the mountains fairly soon, the southern fork seemed the likely course. So positive was he that his judgment was correct, he named the southern fork the Missouri River and the northern fork Maria's River (now the Marias River). The other leader of the expedition, Captain William Clark, agreed with Lewis's decision.

The rest of the Corps of Discovery, as the mission was called, did not share Lewis's opinion. Even after he explained his reasoning, he reported, "The whole of my party to a man . . . were fully persuaded" that the northern route was correct. But the group was still willing to follow its captain loyally even when it thought he was making the wrong decision. Lewis refused to risk the safety of his expedition by splitting up and traveling along both branches of the river. He also did not want to waste any time by sending a small party up one of the branches while the rest of the expedition waited at the fork. But to counter the unanimous opposition, Lewis decided that he would travel with a swift party on foot ahead of the rest along the southern route. The remainder of the group, led by Clark, would be following behind with the supplies. Lewis was eager to find the great falls quickly and reassure the others that the southern route was correct.

RESULT

The small scouting party forged ahead along the southern fork of the river on June 11, while the rest followed behind. Two days later, Meriwether Lewis came across the roaring series of waterfalls that the Hidatsas had described. This convinced everyone that they were indeed on the right track.

When Meriwether Lewis spied the great falls on the Missouri River, he called it "the grandest sight I ever beheld."

After a long delay caused by the difficulty of getting their equipment around the falls, the Lewis and Clark expedition continued along the river until it reached the mountains. The expedition was fortunate to avoid all hostile Indians. And, just when they were most desperate for supplies, they encountered a group of Shoshones led by none other than Sacagawea's brother. As Lewis had hoped, the Shoshones were eager to trade horses for weapons. The horses the expedition obtained from these Shoshones enabled it to cross the mountains. However, finding the Columbia River was not as easy as hoped. The party still had to travel to the north and west quite a way. But eventually they reached it and proceeded toward the Pacific Ocean. On November 7, 1805, Lewis wrote that the expedition was finally "in view of the ocean, this great Pacific Ocean which we [have] been so long anxious to see."

The Lewis and Clark expedition returned safely from its travels and provided the United States government with valuable information about the Louisiana Territory and also the land west of the Rocky Mountains. Within a few decades, enough settlers had made their way into this region that the United States was able to negotiate with Great Britain for ownership of the north-west territory that includes the present-day states of Oregon, Washington, Idaho, and Montana.

ANALYSIS

By holding to his conviction that the southern fork was the correct route, despite the opposition of almost every other member in the party, Lewis saved the expedition from disaster. Had they taken the northern branch, they still would have reached the mountains, which was where Lewis and Clark wanted to go. In fact, as this would have been the shortest route into the mountains, the expedition might have believed they had chosen the correct branch. However, this route would have carried them far to the north of the Shoshones and their horses, which were essential to the party's success. As historian Stephen E. Ambrose notes, "the odds would have been against the men and their captain."

Splitting the expedition in two and having each travel one branch would probably have lured half of the expedition to the likely disaster along the northern route.

Lewis also would have lost time sending a small expedition up one of the rivers while the rest waited at the fork. Had the small expedition gone down the southern branch, it would have found the great falls, but it would have had to return to the fork to tell the others. If it had gone up the northern branch looking for the falls, there is no telling how long it would have been before the party returned disappointed.

8

EXPLORING THE
FROZEN WASTELAND
1911

You are planning a journey to the last unexplored region on earth—the South Pole. Your goal is to be the first person to reach the pole. You will also conduct scientific research along the way. This will be incredibly dangerous because of the brutal climate and terrain. Antarctica is simply not suitable for most forms of life. Except for seals, penguins, and a few other birds that hug the comparatively warm coastline, no animals can survive for long in such a place.

There are no rivers, roads, or even paths in this frozen wasteland. You will have to travel over ice and snow and even cross a mountain range, often in blizzard conditions. You will have to move quickly, since there are

As if your journey weren't difficult enough, you must also cross the Transantarctic Mountain Range. In order to do this, you need to find a glacier (foreground) to use as your mountain pass. The glaciers are fed from a plateau that surrounds the South Pole.

only a few short months in which travel in this region is even thinkable.

Unfortunately, you cannot travel light. Once you get farther in from the coast, you will find no food or natural shelter in this frigid desert. All food must be packed in, as well as tents and fuel for torches to melt snow for water. Unless you can figure out the best way to transport your men and supplies across the snow and ice quickly, you have no hope of surviving this journey.

BACKGROUND

For hundreds of years, Europeans suspected the existence of a southern continent. But because of the harsh sailing conditions around it, explorers never got close enough to Antarctica to actually see it until 1820.

In the nearly 90 years since, several countries, including your homeland, Great Britain, have sent explorers to investigate the continent. Most have stayed near the safety of the coast, but a few have probed hundreds of miles inland. Meanwhile, other explorers have traveled in the bitter cold of the Arctic regions near the North Pole.

These expeditions have used a variety of transportation methods. Many of the Arctic expeditions, and some of the Antarctic ones, have used sleds pulled by dog teams. These dogs are a special breed that are well suited for cold-weather travel. Some polar explorers, primarily the Greenlanders and Norwegians, believe that these dog sleds are the only practical means of long-distance travel in cold weather. They point out that these animals have served usefully for centuries among native Arctic groups.

Dogs work hard under conditions that would kill most other animals. They are also meat-eaters, which is an advantage on a continent where plants do not flourish. Explorers can obtain a fresh supply of meat for dogs by shooting seals and penguins. When that food runs out, as it will in the interior of Antarctica, explorers usually kill some of the weaker dogs and feed them to the remaining ones. On the negative side, sled dogs are compulsive fighters and can be difficult to control.

Some expeditions have used a special cold-weather breed of ponies from Manchuria. These hardy animals are far stronger and better natured than dogs, and they are more easily tamed. In some types of crusty snow, however, their weight causes their hooves to break through the hard surface. The ponies then become bogged down in snow that dogs could easily run over. Furthermore, ponies do not eat meat. All of their food would have to be transported from the ship to the pole and back.

Man-hauling is a British tradition in cold-climate exploration. The British have often found it easier to rely on their own strength and willpower than on unpredictable animals. Their expeditions have traveled hundreds of miles in the Arctic and Antarctic by simply pulling their supplies along the ice on sleds. Besides reliability, this method eliminates the need to bring along extra food for animals. The disadvantage of man-hauling is that explorers travel slower and work harder.

In recent years, inventors have made great strides in developing motorized transportation. Mechanical experts are now at work developing a motorized sled for use in polar regions. The advantages are obvious. Machines can perform a great amount of work without becoming tired. They do not suffer mentally or emotionally in harsh conditions. The fuel they need can be more easily stored and carried than food for dogs or horses.

Motorized sleds, however, can break down. And they do not always run well in extreme cold. No one has ever tried to operate motorized sleds under the numbing conditions in which you will be traveling.

THE DECISION IS YOURS.

Your survival depends on your ability to transport your team across this icy wasteland. A mistake in this cruel climate will wreck your effort to reach the South Pole. It could also easily cost you and your companions your lives. What method of transportation will you choose?

Option 1 Use sled dogs.

Native arctic people know much more about living in cold climates than anyone else. They have used sled dogs for centuries. These dogs are tried and true in these conditions. In contrast, a motorized sled has never been used on a polar expedition. Can you justify risking your men's lives on some experimental technology?

Such famous arctic explorers as Fridtjof Nansen and Robert Peary used sled dogs. They argue strongly that they are essential to polar travel. They can travel much more easily across snow and ice than humans or ponies. Also, if you expend too much energy dragging your own sleds, you increase the risk of suffering from exhaustion. Once that happens out on the Antarctic ice, you will have no chance to rest or recover.

The key to sled dogs is control. Perhaps the British have had trouble with dogs in the past because they simply did not know how to use them. Sled dogs are unique animals. It takes years to understand their nature and their habits and determine how they will best respond to you. If you hire the best dog sled driver you can find, you should be able to keep the dogs in line and working hard for you.

Option 2 Use ponies.

You have to go with what has been used under conditions most similar to those you will face. The fact is that no one has traveled farther in Antarctica than Sir Ernest Shackleton. In traveling to the South Pole, you will be

Ernest Shackleton used horses hitched to sleds on a previous expedition to move supplies and equipment.

going into the very region that Shackleton traveled. What did Shackleton bring along as his main mode of transportation? Ponies.

British explorers have had trouble getting dogs to pull their sleds. They claim that dogs are too wild and ferocious for a trip of such importance. Furthermore, they argue that the use of dogs in the polar regions is inhumane. They see it as unforgivably cruel to run dogs to death and then feed them to their companions just so humans can explore new territory.

Option 3 **Use motorized sleds.**

Subjecting either horses or dogs to such bone-chilling conditions would be inhumane. The explorers are there by choice, but expecting animals to haul thousands of pounds of equipment over the ice is asking too much.

They will have all they can handle just surviving in the cold. The logical solution is to let unfeeling machines bear the brunt of the work.

Skeptics have often scoffed at the use of modern technology and have been proven wrong time and again. Engineers have made great strides in getting machines to work in cold weather. Motor cars have proven reliable even in the cold regions of Canada and Russia.

Mechanics have been working on a new design that uses caterpillar tracks to propel a sled across the ice. In a recent test in Norway, one of these motorized sleds ran all afternoon in the cold without a problem.

The sledge trials in Norway. This latest version of the motorized sled moves over the ice and snow using caterpillar tracks.

Option 4 **Use man-hauling.**

While the motorized sled has run well in a few experiments, it has never been used under the extreme conditions you will face. Even the best new devices often need a lot of refining before they prove reliable. Trusting your expedition to unproven technology is a huge gamble.

This is especially true given the final report of Reginald Skelton, the man who built the motorized sleds to your specifications. Skelton listed more than 60 things that could go wrong with the motors under extreme conditions. Any one of these problems could disable the sled and leave you without transportation.

Since you cannot trust the motors, and since using animals is both unreliable and inhumane, the best course of action is to have your crew haul the equipment manually. This actually could have a beneficial effect, because the effort of pulling heavy loads will keep you warm as you travel during the day. Nor would you have to worry about hauling extra food for the animals.

A number of British expeditions have hauled their supplies for hundreds of miles in arctic conditions on numerous occasions. A recent example of this is the 1,328 miles covered by Lieutenant Leopold McClintock in search of a lost expedition in extreme northern Canada.

Option 5 **Use a combination of all four.**

There are serious potential problems with each of your four transportation options. Dogs are difficult to control. Horses may not be suited to all arctic conditions. Motorized sleds may break down. Man-hauling could exhaust you and your crew.

The best way to insure that your expedition succeeds is to keep all options available. Use the motorized sleds to carry the heavy loads for as long as they run. If the sleds die, you could then turn to horses to do the heavy pulling. Dogs could take over when you come across terrain that you suspect might be difficult for the ponies. When all else fails, turn to man-hauling.

This option provides you with insurance in case one or more of the means of transportation proves faulty. Together, these four methods should be able to move the expedition to the South Pole and back.

The drawback to this option is that it would make the expedition oversized and slow. Should one of these methods prove far superior to the others, you would have to decide whether to switch entirely to that method. You would be forced either to drag along the rest or leave them behind. It may be better to focus on just one of the other methods and perfect it.

YOU ARE THE EXPLORER.
WHAT IS YOUR DECISION?

Option 1   Use sled dogs.

Option 2   Use ponies.

Option 3   Use motorized sleds.

Option 4   Use man-hauling.

Option 5   Use a combination of all four.

No matter which option Robert Scott (1868-1912) chose to move his equipment, he and his men would have to bring along skis to transport themselves over the ice. Scott is shown here fully dressed for polar exploration.

Robert Scott chose *Option 5*.

Scott had little faith in sled dogs. In a previous expedition to Antarctica, he had attempted to use them for travel. But the dogs often refused to pull their sleds and needed frequent rest breaks. Scott also disliked the way they constantly fought with each other. Furthermore, he strongly felt that the practice of sacrificing weakened dogs to feed the stronger ones was inhumane. According to Scott, "Nothing has been done with [dogs] to be compared to what men have achieved without dogs."

From early on, Scott believed that motorized sleds were the key to transporting equipment in Antarctica. But Skelton's report drove home the risk involved in trusting lives to new, untested technology. Scott turned to ponies as his backup. He decided to use the motorized sleds as long as possible, then switch to ponies. These, he hoped, would carry him as far as the great glaciers that rose up in the center of the continent. With the footing likely to be bad for ponies the closer he came to the pole, Scott intended to use man-hauling over the final distance to his goal. "If the motors are successful, we shall have no difficulty in getting to the Glacier," Scott wrote. "If they fail, we shall still get there with any ordinary degree of good fortune."

On the advice of Nansen, Scott reluctantly brought along a small team of dogs as well, although he did not intend to make great use of them. He held the romantic view that man-hauling was more true to the spirit of exploration. It would, he wrote, "make the contest more nobly and splendidly won."

RESULT

After setting up winter camp in 1910 on the Ross Ice Shelf, Scott's team set out to deposit supplies along the path they would take in the spring, when the weather would permit traveling again. This would allow them to resupply themselves without having to haul everything along on their way to the pole and back. Using all four forms of transportation, they plodded off to stash one ton of their supplies. Unfortunately, they lost several horses just doing this.

The Ross Ice Shelf, as seen from Scott's ship in 1910. This ice shelf is so vast in area, it could cover France. And it rises as high as 200 feet in some places.

Upon returning to base, Scott's team was shocked to find that a rival expedition from Norway was on the same ice shelf. Scott and his team had learned about their competition while on their way to Antarctica. But Scott thought the Norwegian team, led by polar explorer Roald Amundsen, was beginning its journey from the less-explored Weddell Sea. Scott had now lost an important advantage and felt he was being intruded upon.

Unlike Scott, Amundsen depended entirely on sled dogs and skis for transportation. In addition, Amundsen's only goal was to be the first at the South Pole. He would not spend time collecting scientific data.

Starting two months later in the season, Amundsen and his dogs were able to store three tons of supplies far closer to the pole than Scott, who was able to move only one-third the amount of supplies.

Exceptionally cold weather lingered into spring 1911. Aware that his horses could not tolerate the conditions, Robert Scott had to delay his start by several weeks. Amundsen also was delayed by the weather, but he was still able to start ahead of Scott. While Scott sat in his camp, the Norwegian expedition and their dogs charged off toward the pole. Amundsen wrote, "Dogs pull magnificently. . . . How men and horses are going to get through in these conditions I cannot understand."

Amundsen's doubts were well founded. The horses sank in snow over their knees and struggled mightily to plow through deep snow drifts. Scott's technology also failed to give him an advantage over Amundsen, as his sleds broke down after just five days. With no expert mechanic available, Scott had to abandon the vehicles.

While the British expedition trudged through the ice and snow, Amundsen forged ahead with his dog sleds. Encountering no major problems, the Norwegians climbed up the steep ridge of a glacier and proceeded to the South Pole. They reached it on December 14, 1911.

By this time, Scott had lost all of his ponies and had sent his dogs back to camp. He and his men were still hundreds of miles from their goal. More than a month would pass before they finally reached the South Pole only to find the Norwegian flag firmly planted.

Frostbitten, exhausted, and disappointed, Scott's party poses for a picture at the pole. (From left to right) Captain Lawrence Oates, Lieutenant Henry Bowers, Scott, Dr. Edward Wilson, and Edgar Evans

Their heroic effort of man-hauling had completely exhausted Robert Scott and his men. The delays and slow travel left them exposed as the tolerable summer conditions faded away. The strain of pulling their own sleds and a shortage of food and fuel caused the deaths of Scott and his companions on their way back—just 10 miles shy of their largest deposit of supplies.

ANALYSIS

In one of his final letters to his friends, Scott blamed misfortune for his sad fate. But for the most part, he had only himself to blame. Although he claimed that both the motorized sleds and ponies performed as well as he had hoped, the truth was they did not.

The Norwegians credited their dogs with providing them a relatively safe trip to the South Pole. "The dogs are the most important thing for us," one said early in the expedition. "The whole outcome of the expedition depends on them." For Amundsen, the idea of pulling his own sleds was ridiculous—though he brought along human harnesses just in case. The Norwegians' success in contrast with the tragic failure of the British proved beyond a doubt the superiority of sled dogs at that time.

Robert Scott was so opposed to using dogs that he brought too few to provide the bulk of his transport and did not make good use of those he had. Scott's mistrust of dogs came from his past experience with them in Antarctica. But his bad experience resulted from the fact that Scott had no one along on his previous trips who knew how to handle sled dogs. He felt it was inhumane to

Roald Amundsen (1872-1928) had devoted almost his entire life to being the first to reach the North Pole. After Robert Peary and Matthew Henson beat him to it in 1909, Amundsen turned his focus south.

make dogs do all the work, and then feed most of them to the few that proved to be the best. Amundsen, on the other hand, arranged to bring along the best sled handlers he could find.

Scott made another mistake in basing his decision to use ponies on Shackleton's opinion. Scott should have paid closer attention to the fact that Shackleton's last pony died long before he reached the farthest point in his failed attempt to reach the South Pole in 1908.

Scott's experiment with motorized sleds might have worked out better had he committed himself more firmly to it. He neglected to bring along spare parts and someone who knew enough about the machines. Skelton, who knew the motors inside and out and was a veteran Antarctic explorer, had pleaded with Scott to be allowed to come. Nonetheless, Scott left him behind. As a result, the first mechanical breakdown spelled doom for the motorized sleds and the beginning of the end for Scott.

The British expedition's tent, as found by a rescue party the following spring. When one of the rescuers looked inside, he wrote, "I saw a most ghastly sight, those sleeping bags with frozen bodies in them; the one in the middle I recognized as Capt. Scott."

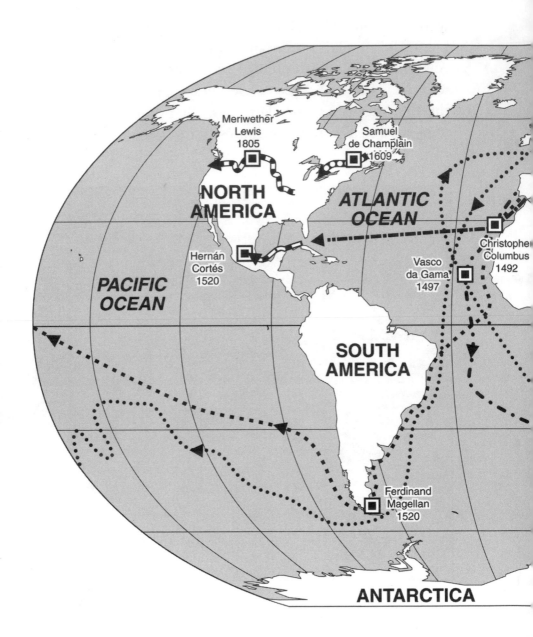

Meriwether
Lewis
1805

Samuel
de Champlain
1609

NORTH
AMERICA

ATLANTIC
OCEAN

Christopher
Columbus
1492

Hernán
Cortés
1520

PACIFIC
OCEAN

Vasco
da Gama
1497

SOUTH
AMERICA

Ferdinand
Magellan
1520

ANTARCTICA

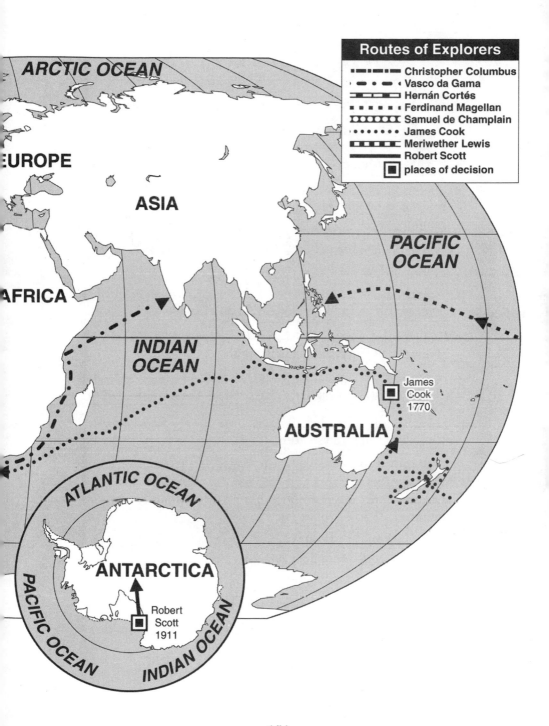

Routes of Explorers

- ▬▬▬ Christopher Columbus
- ●▬●▬● Vasco da Gama
- ▭▭▭ Hernán Cortés
- ▪▪▪▪ Ferdinand Magellan
- ▭▭▭▭ Samuel de Champlain
- •••••• James Cook
- ▪▪▪▪▪ Meriwether Lewis
- ▬▬▬ Robert Scott
- ◼ places of decision

ARCTIC OCEAN

EUROPE

ASIA

AFRICA

INDIAN
OCEAN

PACIFIC
OCEAN

AUSTRALIA

James
Cook
1770

ATLANTIC OCEAN

ANTARCTICA

PACIFIC OCEAN

INDIAN OCEAN

Robert
Scott
1911

Source Notes

Quoted passages are noted by page and order of citation.

pp. 23 (1st), 24: Christopher Columbus, *The Log of Christopher Columbus*, translated by Robert H. Fuson (Camden, Maine: International Marine, 1987).

pp. 23 (2nd), 24-25: Gianni Granzotto, *Christopher Columbus*, translated by Stephen Sartarelli (Garden City, NY: Doubleday, 1985).

pp. 58, 73: Harold Faber, *The Discoverers of America* (New York: Charles Scribner's Sons, 1992).

p. 68: Ian Cameron, *Magellan and the First Circumnavigation of the World* (London: Wiedenfeld and Nicolson, 1974).

p. 77: George Sandelin, *The First Voyage around the World* (New York: Harper & Row, 1966).

pp. 92 (both), 94: Sabra Holbrook, *The French Founders of North America and Their Heritage* (New York: Antheneum, 1976).

p. 111 (all): John Gwyther, *Captain Cook and the South Pacific* (Boston: Houghton Mifflin, 1954).

pp. 119-120, 129, 132: Stephen E. Ambrose, *Undaunted Courage: Meriwether Lewis, Thomas Jefferson, and the Opening of the American West* (New York: Simon & Schuster, 1996).

pp. 130, 131: Bernard DeVoto, ed., *The Journals of Lewis and Clark* (Boston: Houghton Mifflin, 1981).

pp. 143 (1st), 145, 147, 149: Roland Huntford, *The Last Place on Earth* (New York: Antheneum, 1983).

p. 143 (2nd): Reginald Pound, *Scott of the Antarctic* (London: Cassell, 1966).

p. 143 (3rd): Piers Pennington, *The Great Explorers* (New York: Facts on File, 1979).

BIBLIOGRAPHY

Ambrose, Stephen E. *Undaunted Courage: Meriwether Lewis, Thomas Jefferson, and the Opening of the American West.* New York: Simon & Schuster, 1996.

Axelson, Eric. *Congo to Cape: Early Portuguese Explorers.* London: Faber and Faber, 1973.

Bell, Christopher. *Portugal and the Quest for the Indies.* London: Harper & Row, 1974.

Brandon, William. *Indians.* Boston: Houghton Mifflin, 1987.

Cameron, Ian. *Magellan and the First Circumnavigation of the World.* London: Wiedenfeld and Nicolson, 1974.

Columbus, Christopher. *The Log of Christopher Columbus.* Translated by Robert H. Fuson. Camden, Maine: International Marine, 1987.

DeVoto, Bernard, ed. *The Journals of Lewis and Clark.* Boston: Houghton Mifflin, 1981.

Dor-Ner, Zvi, and William G. Scheller. *Columbus and the Age of Discovery.* New York: William Morrow, 1991.

Faber, Harold. *The Discoverers of America.* New York: Charles Scribner's Sons, 1992.

Goetzmann, William H., and Glyndwr Williams. *The Atlas of North American Exploration.* New York: Prentice Hall, 1992.

Granzotto, Gianni. *Christopher Columbus.* Translated by Stephen Sartarelli. Garden City, N.Y.: Doubleday, 1985.

Gwyther, John. *Captain Cook and the South Pacific.* Boston: Houghton Mifflin, 1954.

Hart, Henry H. *Sea Road to the Indies.* New York: Macmillan, 1950.

Holbrook, Sabra. *The French Founders of North America and Their Heritage.* New York: Atheneum, 1976.

Huntford, Roland. *The Last Place on Earth*. New York: Atheneum, 1983.

Jones, Vincent. *Sail the Indian Sea*. London: Gordon & Cremonesi, 1978.

Madariaga, Salvador de. *Hernán Cortés: Conqueror of Mexico*. London: Hollis & Carter, 1942.

Marrin, Albert. *Aztecs and Spaniards: Cortés and the Conquest of Mexico*. New York: Atheneum, 1986.

Matthews, Rupert. *Explorer*. New York: Knopf, 1991.

Morison, Samuel Eliot. *Samuel de Champlain: Father of New France*. Boston: Little, Brown, 1972.

Parr, Charles McKew. *Ferdinand Magellan, Circumnavigator*. New York: Crowell, 1964.

Pennington, Piers. *The Great Explorers*. New York: Facts on File, 1979.

Pigafetta, Antonio. *Magellan's Voyage around the World*. Translated by James Alexander Robertson. Cleveland: Arthur H. Clark, 1906.

Pound, Reginald. *Scott of the Antarctic*. London: Cassell, 1966.

Ronda, James P. *Lewis and Clark Among the Indians*. Lincoln, Nebraska: University of Nebraska Press, 1984.

Sandelin, George. *The First Voyage around the World*. New York: Harper & Row, 1966.

Scheller, William. *The World's Greatest Explorers*. Minneapolis: The Oliver Press, 1992.

Silverberg, Robert. *The Longest Voyage*. Indianapolis: Bobbs-Merrill, 1972.

Thomas, Hugh. *Conquest: Montezuma, Cortés, and the Fall of Old Mexico*. New York: Simon & Schuster, 1993.

Villiers, Alan. *Captain James Cook*. New York: Charles Scribner's Sons, 1967.

INDEX

China, 11, 14, 18, 26, 82
circumference of earth, 13-14
Clark, William, 125, 129, 132.
  See also Lewis and Clark
  expedition
Columbia River, 118, 131
Columbus, Christopher, 49;
  background of, 13, 14, 16,
  19, 22, 23; calculation of, on
  distance to Indies, 14, 18, 21,
  23, 24, 26, 77; crew of, 12,
  14, 16; as Portuguese
  explorer, 14, 22; relationship
  of, with crew, 14-15, 16-17,
  19, 23, 24-25, 26, 63;
  sponsored by Spain, 14, 15,
  16; voyage of, 11-12, 22, 23-
  25, 26, 32
compass, 12
Cook, James: background of,
  110; expedition of, in south
  Pacific, 97-98, 99-100, 110,
  114; maps made by, 97, 100,
  106, 110, 113; objectives of,
  97, 98-99; ship of, grounded
  on coral reef, 98, 100-102,
  103-106, 108, 111; ship of,
  pulled off coral reef, 112
coral reef, 97-98, 100-102,
  103-106, 108, 111, 112, 113
Corps of Discovery, 129. *See
  also* Lewis and Clark
  expedition
Cortés, Hernán: background
  of, 54; confrontation of, with
  Narváez, 55-56, 59;
  conquest of Aztec Empire
  by, 57, 58, 59-60; expedition
  of, to Mexico, 43, 44, 45-46,
  48, 52, 54, 55; gold acquired
  by, 43, 45, 46, 48, 50, 52, 55,
  56, 58, 60; relationship of,
  with Velázquez, 43, 44-45,
  48-49, 54, 55, 59; threatened
  by Narváez, 45, 46, 48, 51, 55
crosstaff, 33

Cruzatte, Peter, 122, 124
Cuba, 44, 48, 54, 55

da Gama, Estêvão (father), 38
da Gama, Vasco: objective of,
  28; route of, 28, 29, 41-42,
  63; ships of, 39, 40, 41;
  voyage of, around Africa, 38,
  39-41, 42
Diaz, Bartolomeu, 27-28, 29-
  30, 33-34, 35, 39, 41
dogs, sled, 135, 136, 137, 138,
  140, 141; used in Amundsen
  expedition, 145, 146, 147,
  148; used in Scott
  expedition, 143, 144, 146,
  147, 148

Endeavor (Cook's ship), 113,
  114, grounded on coral reef,
  98, 100-102, 103-106, 108,
  111; pulled off coral reef,
  112
Euclid, 13
Evans, Edgar, 146
explorer: qualities of, 8-10;
  responsibilities of, 7-8

Ferdinand (king of Spain), 14,
  15, 16
Florida, 8
fothering, 112
France, 90, 116; Champlain as
  representative of, 79, 96; sale
  of Louisiana Territory by,
  117; settlements of, in North
  America, 79, 80-82, 83, 84,
  91, 93, 96; treatment of
  Indians by, 82, 91
fur trade, 82, 84, 88, 91, 93, 94,
  96

Gass, Patrick, 121
gold, 8, 20, 52; acquired by
  Cortés in Mexico, 43, 45, 46,
  48, 50, 52, 55, 56, 58, 60

Quebec, 79, 81, 83, 94
Quetzalcoatl, 45, 46

Rocky Mountains, 115, 131
Ross Ice Shelf, 144, 145

Sacagawea, 119, 120, 121, 131
St. Lawrence River, 79, 81, 82, 91
San Antonio, 73, 74, 77
Scott, Robert: death of, 147, 149; expedition of, through Antarctica, 133-134, 142, 143, 144-147; man-hauling used by, 143, 144, 147; motorized sleds used by, 143, 144, 145, 147, 148-149; ponies used by, 143, 144, 145, 146, 147, 148; rivalry of, with Amundsen, 145-146; sled dogs used by, 143, 144, 146, 147, 148; supplies of, 134, 144, 145, 147
scurvy, 41, 77
Seneca tribe, 87. *See also* Iroquois League of Five Nations
Shackleton, Ernest, 137-138, 148
ships (of exploration): caravel as, 17, 30-34, 35, 36, 37, 39, 41; in fifteenth century, 29, 31; used by Columbus, 14, 17, 23, 32; used by da Gama, 39, 40, 41; used by Magellan, 63, 64, 67, 70-71, 73, 74, 75, 76, 77. *See also Endeavor* (Cook's ship)
Shoshone Indians, 119-121, 122, 131, 132. *See also* Snake Indians
Sioux Indians, 118
Skelton, Reginald, 140, 143, 149
skis, 142, 145
smallpox, 58
Snake Indians, 119-121. *See*

also Shoshone Indians
South America, 42, 61; Magellan's voyage around, 61, 63-65, 66, 68, 69, 73, 77, 78
South Pole, 99, 136, 137, 145, 148; Amundsen's expedition to, 145, 146, 147, 148; Scott's expedition to, 133-134, 141, 143, 144-147
Spain, 26, 55, 68, 70, 75, 92; colonies of, in New World, 44, 55, 58, 80, 84, 117; Columbus sponsored by, 14, 15, 16; explorers sent by, 8, 10, 48, 49, 55, 61; Magellan sponsored by, 61, 63, 66, 69, 70, 71, 72. *See also* Cortés, Hernán
spices, 13, 19, 20, 27, 61, 65, 71
Storms, Cape of, 35, 39

Tenochtitlán, 43, 45, 46, 48, 51-52, 55, 56, 59, 60; siege of, 58, 60
tern, 20
Theatrum orbis terrarum, 4
Tlaxcalans, 45, 52, 58, 59
Transantarctic Mountain Range, 134

United States: Lewis and Clark expedition sent by, 115, 116-117, 131; Louisiana Territory occupied by, 117

Velázquez, Diego, 43, 44-45, 48-49, 54, 55, 59
Vermont, 92
Victoria, 75, 76

Washington, 131
Weddell Sea, 145
Wilson, Edward, 146

ABOUT THE AUTHOR

NATHAN AASENG is an award-winning author of more than 100 fiction and nonfiction books for young readers. He writes on subjects ranging from science to business, government to sports. Aaseng's books for The Oliver Press include *Treacherous Traitors, Great Justices of the Supreme Court, America's Third-Party Presidential Candidates, Genetics: Unlocking the Secrets of Life, Construction: Building the Impossible*, and the nine-volume Great Decisions series including *You Are the President, You Are the President II, You Are the General, You Are the General II, You Are the Supreme Court Justice, You Are the Senator, You Are the Corporate Executive*, and *You Are the Juror*. He lives in Eau Claire, Wisconsin with his wife and children.

Photo Credits

Photographs courtesy of: cover (background, top left, middle left, bottom right), pp. 2, 8, 9, 10, 15, 17, 22, 25, 29, 38, 44, 47, 49, 50, 53, 54, 57, 62, 72, 83, 85, 87, 93, 107, 116, 120, 126, 142, Library of Congress; cover (bottom left, middle right) pp. 81 (NMC-17446), 90 (based on lithograph by Louis C.J. Ducornet/C-6643), 91 (based on painting by C.W. Jefferys/C-103059), 110 (based on painting by N. Dance/C-17726), National Archives of Canada; cover (top right), pp. 119, 125, 128, Minnesota Historical Society; pp. 6, 12, 33, 36, 40, 65, 76, 99, The Mariner's Museum, Newport News, Virginia; p. 13, National Library of Medicine; p. 20, Frederick D. Atwood; pp. 28, 31, 35, 46, 59, 69, 75, 134, 146, Archive Photos; p. 80, *Weapons and Armor* (published by Dover Publications, Inc., 1978); pp. 98, 101, 104, 105, 114, National Library of Australia; p. 113, Collection: John Oxley Library, Brisbane; p. 123, Shane Reno, Montana; p. 130, Haynes Foundation Collection, Montana Historical Society; pp. 138, 139, 144, 149, Scott Polar Research Institute; p. 148, William H. Hobbs Collection, Special Collections Library, University of Michigan.